Career Prescription Guide

A Physician's Guide for Career Transformation or Advancement

Pamela C. Sullivan
MD, MBA, CPE, FACP, FCUCM, PT

AAPL

Published by **American Association for Physician Leadership, Inc.**

PO Box 96503 | BMB 97493 | Washington, DC 20090-6503

Website: www.physicianleaders.org

AAPL books are available at special quantity discounts to use as premiums and sales promotions, or for use in corporate training programs. For more information, please write to Special Sales at journal@physicianleaders.org

This publication is designed to provide general information and is sold with the understanding that neither the author nor the publisher is engaged in rendering legal, accounting, ethical, or clinical advice. If legal or other expert advice is required, the services of a competent professional person should be sought.

13   8 7 6 5 4 3 2 1

Copyedited, typeset, indexed, and printed in the United States of America

PUBLISHER
Nancy Collins

PRODUCTION MANAGER
Jennifer Weiss

DESIGN & LAYOUT
Carter Publishing Studio

COPYEDITOR
Patricia George

DEDICATION

It is my intention to write only one book in my lifetime. Hence, this dedication list is long, but it holds great meaning for me. Feel free to have a chuckle or empathize.

Neil, Casey, Jessica, Brian, Madaket, Easton, Mom, Dad, and Jackie: thank you for being my cheerleaders and number one supporters of my fan club, of which you are the only members.

Dr. Greg Daniels: for opening my first leadership opportunity door.

Nick Loporcaro, Chris Johnson, Dr. Lynn Massingale, and Max Cohen: highly successful CEOs who value people.

Dr. Michael Ammazzalorso (posthumously) and Dr. Michael Le: mentors who supported, not judged.

Dr. Kevin Klauer: a role model with more energy than I, inspiring and influencing physicians worldwide.

Drs. John Pracyk, Kevin Coates, Jasen Gundersen, and PEMBA Class of 2015: a second family.

Sue Salvemini and Kim Linde: inspirations who show me the silver lining.

Dr. John Schufeldt: placed the crazy idea in my head that I should write this book.

Steve Sellars: always takes my calls when I'm in need of an ear to listen.

Tom Brown: whose official title is admissions and alumni manager at the University of Tennessee and without whose unwavering support, many of my PEMBA colleagues would not have MBA after their names.

TABLE OF CONTENTS

ABOUT THE AUTHOR

Pamela Sullivan is a strategic leader, mentor, and consultant with over 30 years of experience in healthcare. Starting her career as a physical therapist, she went on to complete medical school and a residency in internal medicine, followed by a distinguished career in emergency medicine and urgent care. Sullivan served as chief clinical officer at Landmark Health, where she played a pivotal role in leading national clinical operations, building teams, and driving value-based care initiatives, enabling care in the homes of chronically ill patients.

Now, as a consultant to multiple value-based care startup companies, she brings a unique perspective and expertise in clinical integrations, lean process improvement, team development, and operational efficiency. Known for her action-oriented, decisive approach, Sullivan thrives in environments where continuous improvement and positive team culture are prioritized. She is passionate about mentoring emerging healthcare leaders and developing high-performing teams that are aligned with the mission of putting patients first.

A recognized leader in the healthcare industry, Sullivan was the first female president of the Urgent Care Association of America and has served on numerous boards shaping the future of healthcare. She has received several prestigious awards, including the Lifetime Achievement Award from the Urgent Care Association and the Laureate Award from the American College of Physicians. Her desire for continuous improvement stems from a lack of mentors for female physicians early in her career. She views obstacles as opportunities. Her public speaking abilities have landed her on multiple platforms.

Sullivan attributes her success to the unwavering support of her family — her husband, two daughters, son-in-law, parents, and sister — and to those who believed in her by opening doors to new opportunities. A New Yorker for over 50 years, she now lives in Arizona, where she enjoys pickleball, hiking, knitting, cooking, and time with friends.

CONTRIBUTING AUTHORS

The concept for this book is to be practical, allowing you to apply the concepts for your individualized situation. It is not loaded with results of research studies. It is packed with step-by-step guidance, including illustrative stories as real examples. The steps outlined in this book can be applied to any person in any profession, despite the words on these pages being directed toward physicians. The final chapter is a series of vignettes written by physicians "in their own words," taking you through their journeys. Words truly do not express my gratitude for their willingness to share some very personal and emotional times in their lives.

Dr. Priya Radhakrishnan, a phenomenal leader, contributes a poem she wrote on imposter syndrome. Her words have left an enduring impression on how I treat others. Dr. Bahar Sedarati eloquently shares her expertise on mentorship, providing brilliant insights on the subject.

Vignette Contributors:

Jonathan D. Block, MD, MBA, MLS, MPH, CPE
Dr. Anonymous
Philip Horowitz, MD
Kevin Klauer, DO, DJD
Karen J. Nichols, DO, MA, MACOI, MACP, CS-F
Karen Raffery, MD, JD
Felix Reyes, MD, FCCP, FACP
Pedro Rodriguez-Guggiari, MD, FACP
Geogy Thomas, MD, FAAFP, MBA
Ijeoma Uche, MD, PharmD, FACP

Foreword

Career Prescription Guide

Kevin M. Klauer, DO, EJD

All physicians are deemed leaders. Some embrace their leadership roles in healthcare more than others, intentional about seeking those roles, while others may prefer not to lead at all and opt out as quickly as they can. Nonetheless, healthcare delivery would wander aimlessly off track without the guidance of the physician's voice, experience, and breadth of knowledge.

In a similar context, most orchestra conductors are, or have been, instrumentalists. There is a certain logic to the pattern that those who excel as musicians may find themselves conducting, leading others, and "orchestrating" musical and choreographic complexities. The same is true for medicine and healthcare. Administrators, legislators, and the healthcare community as a whole look to physicians for answers, and those recognized for their clinical excellence often find themselves at the top of the leadership short list.

Although physicians and musicians alike may find their way to leadership through performance excellence, that is where their similarities diverge. Defined pathways exist for education and training to lead in the musical arts, yet physicians are often left to their own trial-and-error approach to professional development.

While making your own mistakes may crystallize and solidify critical learnings along your professional development journey, collecting and learning from a montage of errors is inefficient, ill-advised, and a recipe for disaster.

I have known Pamela (Pam) Sullivan for years, witnessed her excellent leadership, and am inspired by her career trajectory. This book, *Career Prescription Guide: A Physician's Guide for Career Transformation or Advancement,* is an outstanding compilation of perspectives, guidance, and exactly what the "doctor ordered" with respect to insightful leadership development.

Put yourself on the fast track to success and read this guide cover to cover.

How Did I Get Here?

RESILIENCE

"Wow! You'll have an MD *and* an MBA. You can do whatever you want!" I heard this often as I was obtaining my MBA. Thoughts of the world opening up opportunities for me, allowing me to control my happiness at work, started to creep into my head. Work was a job. Work paid the bills. Work allowed my family to be happy. Work was what I did because I had a responsibility to do it. But could it be more?

My journey to becoming a physician did not follow the common path. I grew up in the 1960s and 1970s as a "gym rat," spending most of my time in a gymnastics environment. I was never a superstar gymnast; I was just an average gymnast who spent a lot of time in the gym — which happened to be the family business. My dad, who had an MBA and several other degrees, started the gym from scratch. He had no experience with gymnastics or running a business, but I learned a lot from him.

Each generation has its "norms" for expectations. When I was growing up, if you were smart, you became a lawyer or a doctor. I did not consider myself to be smart, especially compared to my sister, so for me, in 1981, it made sense to go to college to be a physical therapist. After all, gymnasts often end up with a variety of injuries.

Fast-forward four years. I graduated from college in 1985 with a bachelor of arts in physical therapy (which was all that was required for licensure). I started to practice and almost instantly wanted to pursue my master's in physical therapy. Unfortunately, in those days, you needed two years of experience as a physical therapist before you could obtain a master's degree. On top of that, I wanted to specialize in sports medicine. Sports were mostly male-dominated at the time, and a woman was not welcome in the locker room.

"Value-based care" was not yet a buzz phrase. I was disillusioned that I needed a written order by a physiatrist to ambulate a post-op orthopedic patient, which meant that patients who had surgery on Friday had to wait until Monday to get out of bed. It was frustrating. I'd gone to school for four years and had to wait to have someone tell me what I already knew! For the first time in my life, I recognized that I was as smart as the doctors.

At the same time, my sister was graduating from medical school. She believed I had the brains and the abilities to make a great physician and encouraged me to apply to medical school. Thus, after having spent less than a year as a practicing physical therapist, in 1986, I started the journey to becoming a physician.

Several medical schools returned my application along with the application fee, stating that they would not consider me, as I already had a degree in PT. However, I landed a spot on a "waiting list" at a school located across the country.

Two weeks prior to the start of classes, a secretary in the physical therapy department told me I had a phone call. I slipped into a nearby supply closet to take the call on a hard-wired phone hanging on the wall and heard, "You have been accepted to Medical College of Pennsylvania's class of 1990. Will you be able to attend classes starting two weeks from today?"

At that moment, I didn't recognize this was the start of the sinusoidal, up-and-down emotional rollercoaster that one takes throughout their career. I just felt elated and on cloud nine! I'm still grateful that I remained in the moment for at least a few minutes after I'd called my family. I resigned from my job, packed up my apartment, and drove cross-country, arriving fewer than 24 hours before my first day of classes.

Off to Medical School

I worked part-time as a physical therapist while in med school and was shocked when I was asked to be a TA for an anatomy class. My knowledge in this area had been recognized! I declined the offer but did spend extra time in the cadaver lab helping classmates.

Although my plan was to be a sports medicine orthopedic surgeon, I was nervous when we started to choose our specialties. How could I be a great surgeon if I didn't know the basics of managing a patient's diabetes or hypertension? I opted for a residency in internal medicine and planned to follow it up with an orthopedic residency.

In my second year of residency, my orthopedic surgery passion grew, and I began applying to change residency tracks. Feeling dejected that I hadn't yet matched in orthopedics, I tried to cheer myself up by attending a Triple-A baseball game. Remember that sinusoidal emotional rollercoaster? That game was when — at my lowest point — I met the man who became my husband.

The following year, as I reapplied to ortho residencies, only ranking my top five choices, I accepted a one-year position in the emergency department to bridge the gap between completing my residency in internal medicine and starting an ortho residency. Once again, I didn't match.

My quest for an orthopedic residency was challenging — in great measure because I am female. For example, I had to remove my engagement ring at interviews. At that time, residency programs didn't want to take the chance on a woman who was more likely to get pregnant during residency and disrupt the program. I was asked how much I could bench-press, yet the male applicants were not subjected to the same questioning. One interview had me take a 3-D mechanical test like the males did; however, my test had three extra pages because, as it was explained to me, "women are not as mechanically inclined" and I needed to show I understood special relationships and would be able to visualize and perform orthopedic procedures. I received a phone call from one program asking me why I hadn't ranked them — they "needed a skirt" in their program, they explained. Times have definitely changed!

My Development as a Leader

I'm not sure why I didn't appreciate the significance of how I was treated, but I shook it off and moved forward, working in a Level 2 high-volume trauma emergency department for the next 18 years while my husband and I raised two amazing daughters.

My husband and I decided that we wanted to have a parent at home with our daughters to support them throughout the day. My husband, a master carpenter, became a stay-at-home dad and worked harder than I did! He was the chef and the taxi driver, filling every void as I pursued my career.

Over the years, I have been on or chaired many committees. I served on the hospital medical board of a large hospital for over eight years. I tried to position myself so that others would see the value I brought outside of day-to-day patient care. I struggled to find a balance between providing for my family and achieving a sense of job stability at work.

I'll be the first to admit that my leadership skills needed significant polishing. During an annual review, my direct supervisor told me that my comments were always right on point but that I needed to learn how to state them in a more politically correct manner. For a long time, I was blind to my shortcomings; I thought I was positioning myself well, even though I wasn't getting the roles I applied for. **Lesson learned: I needed to increase my emotional intelligence.**

I asked for a mentor. My request was often met with laughter, as there were no mentors specifically for female leaders. So, I went to the chief nursing officer, whom I saw as a confident, exceptional leader. I was surprised when she shared that she'd had a hard time finding a mentor or role model as well. She recommended I read Dale Carnegie's *How to Win Friends and Influence People*. I did, and that started a pivotal change in my thinking. At that time my EQ was not very high, and this book helped me connect the dots and think more like a leader. But I still had a long way to go on my leadership journey.

Years and many CEOs later, a CEO came along who initiated a large-scale, organized change in leadership throughout the hospital, replacing longtime, established leaders. I understood the need for change but had a tough time reconciling that need with the emotional ties I had to the people who had dedicated their careers to the hospital. I asked the CEO how he could make such a decision. I'm grateful that he took the time to explain that he had to do what was right for the business, even if it wasn't popular.

A year later, it became obvious that the CEO thought it was *my* time to leave. I took a position in a competitor's emergency department, only to go through a leadership change and be told I would be replaced as soon as they could hire someone who was trained in emergency medicine. My daughter was heading to college, and I needed a long-term, stable job.

Another Door, Another Opportunity

As the saying goes, when one door closes, another opens. Dr. Greg Daniels took a chance on me, hiring me as a medical director for a newly opened urgent care center. When the center surpassed its business goals significantly earlier than expected, Dr. Daniels rewarded me and three other leaders in the company with a trip to the annual Urgent Care Association of America convention.

It was sheer luck that I sat next to the president of the Urgent Care Association at one of the convention sessions. He didn't introduce himself as the president, and I didn't know who he was at the time. He did ask my opinion about the meeting, and my experience with the New York chapter of the American College of Physicians during my residency allowed me to answer somewhat intelligently. He asked me to run for a position on the board of the Urgent Care Association. One year later, I was elected to serve on that board.

But let's jump back to my role in Dr. Daniel's company. We were opening another urgent care center and had hired a medical director when the town held up our building permits. I'd already taken just under a 50% pay cut when I moved from emergency medicine to urgent care, and I needed to supplement my income to support my family.

This company for which I was employed, Exigence Group, had many business lines, including staffing emergency departments. I had been working shifts to fill staffing gaps at one emergency department and was asked to serve as its medical director. I agreed, as we were in negotiations to sell the company, and taking on the position would stabilize the company's contract with this hospital system during the ongoing negotiations. I was expected to fill the role for six months while maintaining my role as medical director of the urgent care center. The company sold, but I stayed on as the medical director of both facilities for almost four years.

Accelerated Leadership Development

It became obvious that I needed more skills in the business world if I wanted to continue down my leadership path. At the age of 50, I obtained a physician executive MBA. It was the best experience of my career to that point! It was engaging, energizing, and a ton of work. Once again, I had the full support of my family. The hardest call I ever had to make was to Dr. Daniels to tell him that I was resigning my role as urgent care medical director. I couldn't be an effective full-time medical director at two facilities over 100 miles apart while obtaining a one-year accelerated MBA. His response was simply "What took you so long?" I was so relieved to have his support.

My leadership journey was gaining speed. I became the first female president of the Urgent Care Association. When I walked into the first board of directors meeting as president, it was a much different feeling than entering the room as a board member. I felt overwhelmed just thinking about being there surrounded by such highly successful business individuals. I learned so much that year!

At the end of that year, I hand-wrote notes to each board member thanking them for their service to the association and for helping me on my journey. I was surprised when many shared that despite their success, they would not have been as successful in my role because the skills that were needed as president of the board at the time didn't fall into their niche. **Lessons learned: Make others feel their value.**

Remember the CEO who replaced me many years earlier? I was upset when I became one of the "victims, "yet several years later, I met with that CEO and shook his hand, thanking him for changing the trajectory of my career. I would not be where I am today if he hadn't forced me to make a change. He was grateful when I told him that! No one else had shared their appreciation with him.

Leadership as a Journey

I methodically interviewed for new roles after graduating with my MBA. A year later, I accepted a position at a company where I embraced the mission and whose values aligned with mine. I am grateful for that opportunity, as each year I was provided greater leadership opportunities in a wonderful culture. I have proven that I can meet KPIs, reduce costs, and bring value. With an MD and an MBA, I'll have many options as I move forward. This is where the fun begins!

I suspect you're reading this book because you have the drive to advance or change your career. Look back at your own journey. Why did you choose your career starting path? Where did you excel? In retrospect, were there times when you were blinded to clues about where you needed to pivot or gain new skills? Did you stay in a job where you weren't happy, and if you did, why? We'll examine each of these questions (and others) in future chapters.

Why Are You Considering a Change?

CONTEMPLATION

There comes a time when you ask yourself, "What am I doing here? Is this the right job for me? Is the grass greener somewhere else?" Maybe you had a bad day and it's just a fleeting thought... or maybe that fleeting thought starts to replay with increasing frequency in your head.

Most of us have been there at one time or another. However, at some point, you need to stop asking yourself those questions and recognize that what you might need is a career transformation. That's the first step. The second step is thinking about why you want to make a change. Do you want to make a change for a "defendable" reason, or are you working from an emotional response?

A Gallup poll completed in February 2025 revealed that employees in general, not limited to physicians, are seeking new job opportunities at the highest rates since 2015. A survey of 10,342 employees in the United States investigated the top reasons influencing the desire to look for a new employment position. The results revealed 59% of respondents are searching for greater work-life balance, 54 % desire greater overall compensation, 54% are looking for better job security, and 48% want the opportunity to perform at what they do best. Let's explore some of the common reasons you might want to make a career change.

You believe it's expected of you.

You're smart, so others expect you to be employed in a career that requires "brains." In my generation, for example, you were expected to be a doctor or a lawyer if you finished at the top of your class. Maybe you have a certain skill set, like being artistic or musically inclined, so people expect you to pursue a career path that matches your skills. That niche skill may be something you thoroughly enjoy.

For some, however, that special skill can become a burden due to other people's expectations. You may have a great voice but not enjoy singing in public.

Your happiness is the most important happiness, so if the expectations held by others don't make you happy, think long and hard about going down that route. The fear that you'll disappoint someone by choosing a different path shouldn't stop you from going in a direction you'll enjoy. Also keep in mind that what you think other people expect of you may not be accurate. Perceptions are often not the truth. A discussion with the individual(s) you believe you are disappointing can lift a great weight off your shoulders!

Let me provide an example of this based on my own experience. Dr. Daniels provided me with an opportunity, yet I decided to leave that role for financial reasons: I'd been accepted into an MBA program, and I couldn't maintain a full-time position as a medical director in both an urgent care setting *and* in an emergency department. With college tuition looming for me and both of my daughters, I chose to resign the urgent care role and keep the emergency department medical director position because it offered a higher salary.

I was very nervous and upset, thinking I was letting Dr. Daniels down by leaving my urgent care directorship. I called him and, in a shaky voice, told him my decision, dreading what he would say. I was so surprised by his response! "What took you so long?" he asked me. "I've been waiting for you to get your MBA!" You might likewise be surprised when you find out that you're not disappointing somebody, after all!

Maybe staying in the family business is expected of you. It's hard to turn your back when someone has worked so hard to grow a business in the expectation that you'll take it over someday. This is a difficult conversation for sure, but keep in mind the common theme running throughout this book: Be honest with yourself when you answer the question of "What really makes me happy?" You have one life to live. You should not wake up each morning and do something that doesn't support your personal well-being.

Something excites you.

What excites you may become your passion. Suppose you just lost 100 pounds and started training for a marathon. You want to help others with their weight loss and fitness journeys; however, you are a geriatrician. You may feel like you don't have the requisite skill set for this new area of interest. Don't let that dissuade you! Dedication and hard work will get you there in most cases.

Okay, if you're 40 years old and you want to be an Olympic gymnast, maybe you'll need to think twice about your goal. But perhaps becoming a coach or an athletic trainer who supports gymnasts or opening a gymnastics school could be your path.

I bring up this example because I have a friend who wanted to be an Olympic gymnast, but he wasn't the most innately talented gymnast. Still, he worked harder than any other gymnast in the gym. He started running every day. He didn't love running, but he knew it would help him reach his goal. Guess what! He became a gold-medal Olympic gymnast. No matter what your passion, I encourage you to reach for the stars with a well-thought-out plan. A high school basketball coach, Tim Notke, said "Hard work beats talent when talent doesn't work hard."

You're looking for a challenge.

As professional soccer player Peter Shilton said, "If you stand still, there's only one way to go, and that's backwards." If everything around you is evolving while you stay static, you'll fall behind the pack.

Mind you, stasis can be great for some. When I first became a medical director in an emergency department, I wanted to support my team, so I asked each of them to develop their own SMART goals, with the intention of helping them create plans to achieve those goals. One physician explained that he was happy to come to work each day, provide high-quality patient care throughout his 12-hour shift, and then go home. He had no desire to do more than he'd been doing for the past 20-plus years.

I needed about six more people just like him to fully staff the emergency department with great physicians! Worker bees stabilize the company, especially those who promote a positive culture. And they often don't resign when they feel valued. Being content with where you are is a perfectly acceptable plan. I respect an individual who recognizes that a static trajectory is their happiness.

Personally, I get bored if I stay in one place for too long. My job responsibilities changed every year at my last job, which I held for more than six years. Those changes kept me engaged and allowed me to spread my wings by growing my leadership skills. I also know that I enjoy building a new program more than I enjoy maintaining it. You may have the opposite personality. You may enjoy putting out fires and challenging yourself with different opportunities, or you may relish stabilizing standard workflows. All the various personalities and functions serve much-needed niches for overall company success.

You have financial obligations.

This subset of reasoning is multifaceted. First, most people would gladly accept more money for their contributions in the work environment, and usually, the greater the responsibility, risk, or accountability is, the greater the compensation package. This may be exactly what you're looking for as your next steps.

My son-in-law, for example, started his digital marketing career by working for a nonprofit organization. He expanded his skill sets and grew in the role. Years later, he realized that many of his colleagues with similar or even less experience than he had were earning almost double what he was earning by working at for-profit firms. He was at a crossroads. He and my daughter were starting a family, which comes with added expenses. His decision on whether to change careers teetered on whether to be bored but comfortable in his present position or enter a foreign world with higher pay. He chose the latter and quickly recognized that he could excel in his new role.

For those who have a military background, the VA health system is attractive. Benefits, especially retirement benefits, are very hard to match by other organizations. The hours are more regular. This may or may not be a reason to gravitate toward this option. The financial gains should certainly be considered, but will 30–40 years in this setting be the right match for your career?

For my part, I attended a physician executive MBA program. Imagine a class of pediatricians, internists, emergency department physicians, orthopedists, neurosurgeons, and other disciplines — all of us were earning a nice salary. Then we added an MBA to our armamentarium. Common sense says we should therefore be worth more, but in many aspects, we actually were worth *less* if we wanted administrative roles because we didn't have any administrative experience, and clinical patient care drives measurable revenue. That meant some of us had to start lower down the administrative ladder than we'd hoped.

The downstream impact of the return on investment that an administrative physician brings is harder to measure and often not appreciated. It is much simpler to account for the revenue generated by a specific procedure performed by a physician. Numbers on a page are more objectively measured.

As a rule, physicians bring in more money for their institutions when they bill for face-to-face patient care. Taking an administrative role negates this profitability. Hence, administrators receive lower salaries. That pendulum is starting to move in the other direction, however, as it has become increasingly obvious that physician executives can make many businesses more profitable. But going this route does take time, as you typically cannot simply walk into a CEO position. Some of my classmates from my MBA studies remained in patient care, instituting more efficient workflows and improving the profitability of their practice via those means, while others changed career paths or assumed more executive leadership positions.

Money talks… or does it? Throwing money at you may entice you to say yes to an offer, but remember, money does *not* buy happiness. My friend, who's an executive coach, asked me, "What was the last job that made you happy?" At the time, I was holding on to a position that I did not look forward to going to, but the salary was good and allowed my family to buy what we needed and wanted. I could dream of a different job, sure, but I was responsible for my family.

My friend tried to explain to me that my family and I would learn to get by with less income. Still, I had a hard time processing her message until I accepted a job I looked forward to going to each day…and I was making about 60% of my prior salary. I gained confidence and thrived in my new environment. In two separate medical director roles, I queried my team as to what tangible entities would bring them greater job satisfaction. I fully expected higher salaries to be the leading answer. It was not. They almost unanimously declared recognizing a patient's gratitude meant more than an increase in their salary. I devised programs that allowed this gratitude to reach our care teams.

If you had your education subsidized in exchange for working in an underserved area, the requirement to fulfill the terms of the loan may constrain your career options until you meet the obligations associated with that loan.

Everyone has a different level of financial risk tolerance, and that tolerance changes throughout their careers. For example, if you start your own business, you may be taking a financial risk. Your business may be a great success, and you may become a self-made multi-millionaire, or your business may fail. At the same time, owning your own business gives you control. In other words, saying "I have financial reasons" clearly is not *just* about money. (In the next chapter, *What's Stopping You*, we'll discuss why money may hold you back from making a change. Money is a powerful motivator, for better and for worse!)

You have family reasons.

Your next steps professionally and personally might be in conflict. For example, relocating for a desirable job may not be an option because you rely on family to help care for your children, or you are caring for an elderly parent. Maybe you don't want to relocate until your children have graduated from high school. Perhaps your spouse enjoys where you live now and does not want to relocate. Couples contemplating having a family or those who already have young children face other challenges, such as moving to a community that best supports their child's needs and educational development.

Physicians tend to have a higher rate of divorce and relationship issues because of work-related hours and dedication to patients. A trauma surgeon who must spend some nights in the hospital taking call returns home too exhausted to socialize at events a spouse may want to attend. Overtime can wear down a relationship. Decisions need to be made to strengthen the relationship, move on from the marriage, or continue with the status quo. It is not a black and white decision, career versus spouse.

Exploring acceptable options may solve the conflict. Maybe the trauma surgeon opts to perform general surgery only, alleviating the in-house overnight call requirement and the stress of a higher-than-average litigation risk. This same surgeon may go in the direction of employment for a medical device company or one of many other alternatives. My husband and I made the conscious decision to place the children's needs first. This included me being the financial support and becoming a nocturnist, working nights only, which afforded the opportunity for me to attend our children's events during "regular" hours of the day. We dedicated a week every year for a vacation, just the two of us, to re-energize our relationship.

Every family must decide what's right for them when it comes to how to raise their family and have a work-life balance. No one — man or woman — should feel guilty for deciding to devote more time to their family over their career. Do you want to be known for your successes at work or the time you spent with your family and friends? You cannot get back lost time with family.

You may opt to change to an entirely different career or step down from a highly regarded administrative role in order to bring balance to your life. Your spouse may have a hard time understanding your decision to "take a step backward" or give up a highly regarded profession. Their reaction might stem from a fear of changing from a place of comfort to one of unknown stability; they may be dealing with their own loss of identity as the spouse of someone who has a certain elevated position. If you find yourself in this situation, communicate! Help them understand that your decision is *not* a step backward but rather a step in the right direction, one that meets your needs.

Take time to research and educate yourself about opportunities. Explore gaps in your skill sets and work to close them. Building up your résumé with value-added outcomes never hurts! And, COVID brought some good changes in the form of opportunities to work remotely or in hybrid work models.

Your reasons are related to geography.

Geography can play a role in career decisions. You or your family members may have ties to a specific region or want to move to a different climate. One region may have more professional or cultural options than another. For example, have you ever wanted to live in a big city, like New York, filled with museums, restaurants, and cultural activities? This may be your chance. Consider what opportunities are at your fingertips after your workday concludes. Do you want a warm climate, or do you prefer being able to get in a few runs on the ski slopes whenever possible?

A medical student classmate returned home to a very rural setting. He knew he'd be expected to care for injury and illness for which he did not have the expertise, so he learned as he practiced, checking medical books at the patient's bedside. The medical malpractice risk was negligible in this setting. His community of patients was grateful for access to a physician, and he was thankful to practice medicine in a setting he loved.

Each geographic location may have a discrete patient population. A Beverly Hills-like city may be the right geographic location if you want to practice cosmetic plastic surgery in an affluent neighborhood. Beverly Hills should not be your first choice if you want to help underserved inner city populations where there is a totally different payor mix.

Some medical conditions yield better outcomes in certain environments. If your spouse has multiple sclerosis affected by extremes in temperature, that can inform where you practice. Hobbies that provide much-needed mental health benefits, such as skiing or surfing, may guide where you settle. Fortunately, physicians can practice almost anywhere; unfortunately, some physician non-clinical career paths may limit geographic possibilities.

You hate what you're doing.

If you're not happy at your present job and want to get away from it, think about what factors are contributing to your unhappiness. They may include some of the following:

- Poor organization management.
- A long commuting time.
- Long work hours.
- Excessive on-call expectations.
- The amount of work that follows you home.
- The need to be in the office full-time.
- A lack of social contact with colleagues if you're working remotely.
- Feeling undervalued.
- A lack of support.
- Poor benefits.
- A lack of mobility.
- A lack of trust.
- Inadequate salary.
- A culture that doesn't match your own.
- Personal values that do not align with the mission or purpose of the company or institution.
- Not being challenged.
- Disillusionment with the profession overall.
- Feelings of powerlessness to influence or incite change.
- Staffing shortages.
- Lack of financial resources to invest in updated equipment.

Keep in mind that the grass is not always greener on the other side! It may *appear* to be better, but often a different work environment may in fact have similar issues (or different issues that are equally frustrating).

Once you identify the core issue, determine whether you truly dislike the job or if what you dislike is a factor that you may be able to change. For example, maybe you would prefer a hybrid work environment. You won't know if a part-virtual arrangement is possible if you don't ask. There may be potential to participate in direct face-to-face patient care 50% of the time and perform tele-medicine visits the other 50% of the time.

It's critical to determine the *true* reason for your unhappiness; otherwise, history might repeat itself, leading to greater frustration, resentment, and burnout. In the chapter "It's a Big World Out There" I elaborate on how you may be able to manipulate your present environment to accommodate your needs without leaving your present job.

Being a person who likes to be in charge lends itself to starting your own practice or business. But owning a business can mean you are accountable to investors, leaving you with less autonomy than you may desire. The time commitment, necessary skills, and other factors may be right in your wheelhouse or may be overwhelming. We dive into how your personality affects your choices in the chapter "Greatest Strength Equals Greatest Weakness."

You're a lifelong learner.

Most of us are lifelong learners; some people make a career out of it. Some people have badges with more letters after their name than letters in their name. While there's nothing wrong with that, don't get stuck in the trap of thinking that more degrees and credentials will get you that "top" job. They will not. Yes, some jobs have basic academic requirements, but your experience and your proven track record will be the most significant factors when someone makes the decision about who to hire. We dive deeper into this topic in the chapter "Is MD or DO Enough?"

If your focus is lifelong learning, academia may be your cup of tea. A setting that allows you to do research or take on a teaching role may be your destiny.

You feel stressed or overwhelmed.

You may enjoy your job and still need a break. Burnout is real. Fortunately, it's more acceptable these days to admit that you need a mental health break. Depending on your work environment, you may be able to decrease your hours, use personal time off, or secure a lengthy family medical leave based on FMLA. I cannot stress enough how important it is to get help for your mental health. It is *not* a weakness to admit burnout! The opposite is in fact true: It's a strength to recognize burnout; it's a weakness *not* to seek help.

You may be burned out to the point where a shorter-term solution won't be the answer. Physicians — especially those in high-risk areas — sometimes lose the thrill of performing in their domains. It takes a certain degree of emotional intelligence to recognize burnout and determine you need a career change — after all, your identity is tied to your profession. I'll use one of my friends as an example. She was a colorectal surgeon who opted to stop doing surgeries yet continue as a colorectal practitioner, performing office evaluations and nonoperative procedures. She gave up her day-to-day routine because she was burned out as a surgical colorectal physician and a single mom. Likewise, two of my MBA classmates left their surgical careers to pursue other options in the medical field. Adapting from a clinical to a non-clinical role is discussed further in the chapter "It's a Big World Out There."

Consider geographic location when soul-searching for your next steps. Having the ability to hike, mountain bike, kayak, take art classes, or engage in out-of-work activities that bring you joy could solve some of the burnout you are experiencing.

Your health is a factor.

You do not plan your career expecting an unforeseen health-related event to affect your career. Consider an orthopedic surgeon who has a stroke that limits mobility in their arm despite having a sharp mind. Perhaps you are a breast cancer survivor and have a new interest in developing comprehensive breast cancer clinics for patients. Maybe a near-death experience during a heart attack or after a motor vehicle accident prompted a physician to re-evaluate their priorities.

You could not have forecasted any of these circumstances when you were a resident looking toward your future. These events may prompt you to take a leap of faith with your career in a direction you may not have otherwise contemplated. I never realized how happy I would be leaving a healthcare system to pursue a job backed by a private equity company until I looked back in retrospect. These events may ignite you to pursue your passion in a way you never considered otherwise.

There's a merger or acquisition.

A merger or acquisition raises numerous questions. Will I still have a job? Will my salary or benefits change? Will the job expectation change? Will the support systems change? Will I be asked to do more with fewer resources? Will the leadership change? Do I need to learn new workflows and software programs? How will the culture be impacted? You may feel as if the rug had been pulled out from underneath you without notice.

Before running fast in the opposite direction, ask many questions to better understand the intent and impacts. It will take several years for the two companies to truly become one. Often, shared services such as people management, IT, and compliance are the first to integrate, followed by other departments. As you examine the inner workings of this new company, you may decide whether it is or is not for you. Be objective as you analyze your decision. Always have an updated resume!

You are considering pre-retirement.

You may be ready to start tapering down your medical career. You may be looking to travel more, develop hobbies, or enjoy a more leisurely lifestyles. If you aren't ready for full retirement, beware of opportunities that on the surface appear less labor-intensive but that may, in reality, be more stressful or time-consuming. Taking a few days to shadow someone in the role can be insightful or eye-opening.

As a mentor, I recommend formulating a list of three viable options, weighing the risks and benefits of each, and then focusing on the best option when problem-solving. I share the following example:

A medical director, whom I was mentoring, advised me that he had no choice but to place a physician recently hired to practice in a difficult-to-fill position on a PIP (performance improvement plan).

He expressed concerns that the physician was not available to other team members for consultation and his charts were not completed in a timely manner. Over the next few hours, the medical director formulated more than 10 options for going forward. These options ranged from doing nothing to terminating the physician. He engaged the three most viable options, constructing a risk/benefit list of each option.

It became clear to him that termination was not his best option recognizing the cost of replacing the physician, the drain on the rest of the team and himself to take call and double down on the workloads to care for patients, provide guidance to the patient care team himself, and the time away from home as this medical director would need to travel to cover this new hire physician's territory until a replacement physician was hired additionally taking time away from his medical director obligations. The three final options, the risks and benefits of each option, and his final recommendation was presented to his operational dyad partner.

His preparation led to a constructive conversation and earned him respect from his dyad partner for his objective approach to the issue. Ultimately, he worked with the physician to understand his behavior better, formulating a plan to address concerns in concert with the physician. The physician assumed some responsibility while the medical director coached the physician. Satisfactory performance was obtained, avoiding the emotional response of a likely termination as the easiest way to deal with a problem.

IN SUMMARY:

1. Numerous factors may influence your deliberation on making a career change.
2. Objectively weigh the factors that may be impacting your emotions for change.
3. Determine if these elements that create job dissatisfaction can be modified to a more appealing outcome.
4. Being objective will safeguard you from making impulsive decisions, leading you down a path with good intentions but often resulting in unsatisfying outcomes.

5. Consider a palette of options before you become laser-focused on your career future.

What's Stopping You?

CONFLICT

Perhaps you keep thinking about making a change, but you're stuck in a rut. Objectively, you recognize a change is the correct path to take. You want to take action; maybe you've even discussed your situation with a mentor, family member, or friend. But you recognize the opportunities just aren't right for some of the following reasons:

- There's nothing available with my skill sets.
- I should only accept an offer that pays more than my present job.
- I don't want to relocate.
- The drive is too long.
- I don't like the hours.
- I read on Glassdoor that many employees are not happy at the company
- They don't offer remote employment.
- They don't offer flexible scheduling.
- I don't know if I have the skills to do that job.
- The grass isn't always greener on the other side.
- The devil I know is better than the devil I don't know.
- You have J-1 Visa restrictions.
- I cannot abandon my team. They need me.

And the list goes on and on…

You need to be honest with yourself. Do you really want to make a change, or are you making excuses consciously or unconsciously? You may genuinely believe that you want to make a change, but deep down, something is holding you back. These unconscious thoughts or emotions may be difficult to pinpoint. Take the time to sort through this phase. Compare the process to seeking insights from a therapist. It will take more than one session to fully achieve your desired endpoint. This voyage is just as important as or more important than the destination. Let's look at some potential unrecognized reasons why you may be stuck in quicksand:

- You have a fear or a high degree of discomfort with the unknown.
- You lack confidence.
- You have existing obligations.
- You're comfortable where you are today; change is overwhelming.
- You don't have any role models.
- Your skill sets aren't suitable for the new role.
- You don't have enough support to move forward.
- You have a sense of loyalty to your current job/company.
- You like the title but not the job.
- You are competing against your spouse/partner.
- You are restricted for one reason or another.
- You have experienced the arrival fallacy in the past.
- You have not clarified your personal values.

Let's explore each of these reasons separately, understanding that you may have several reasons for resisting or feeling ambiguous when it comes to a career change. There's some overlap with fine differences between each subject discussed in the subsequent section.

You have a fear of the unknown.

I am sure you have heard the term "a fish out of water" or a "stranger in a strange land." You rightfully feel out of place in a new role. As a medical student and as a resident, you were closely supervised initially. During each year of residency, you took on more and more responsibility, gaining increased independence. You certainly did not have the same degree of confidence on your first day of internship as you did on your last day of residency. Likewise, your first day as a full-fledged practicing physician, I suspect, was intimidating to varying degrees. Through each of these progressive steps from medical student to resident to attending physician, you transitioned from discomfort to a sense of comfort and security.

There are many ways to combat this initial uncomfortable feeling. First, acknowledge that you would not have been offered a contract if your hiring manager did not believe you could do the job. Next, find out if your new position has a supportive orientation program. I remember a time when we would bounce around from hospital to hospital, staffing one emergency department after another. The orientation consisted of knowing where the crash carts were located and ensuring you had a login for the computer with access to the radiology software. Job satisfaction, performance metrics, and patient complaints all improved after we instituted a comprehensive standardized orientation at multiple national companies.

Request an opportunity to shadow someone with a similar role. Shadowing will enhance your understanding of the culture and workflows within a company. Key contact introductions are a must. Ask questions for greater understanding. Do not make assumptions.

Mentorship clearly has positive impacts on your development. We examine this topic in the chapter "Mentorship and Coaching."

You lack confidence.

My daughter was two days away from starting nursing school when she began to question her decision. "What if I fail?" she asked me. I said, "You will have tried, and just by trying, you will have *not* failed." She feared nursing school because she didn't have confidence in her ability to make the change from working as a vet tech to becoming a nurse.

I asked her how she had felt the first time she monitored anesthesia on a dog having surgery. "Nervous," she replied. I asked how she feels about monitoring anesthesia on animals now. "Bored! It's so easy." It became clear to her that as she developed confidence in her new skills, she would succeed. Today, my daughter has her nursing degree and excels in a Level 1 emergency department. Many view requesting help as a sign of weakness. I consider it a sign of strength. It is likely that others already see areas where you falter. Addressing them head-on by asking for help should garner respect.

I have instilled this culture of requesting and providing support in many work environments. Consider, for example, a nurse practitioner or physician assistant who is caring for patients in the home. Yes, they are the sole care providers on any given visit; however, I want that advanced practice provider to know they are not alone. If they have a question about how to manage a patient or situation, they have me as the collaborative practice physician (or resource) or maybe an entire interdisciplinary team behind them. The overarching goal is excellence in patient care. That advanced practice provider should feel comfortable about asking for help. They should not feel like they have failed themselves or the patient.

Many physicians resisted the change from paper charts to electronic medical charts due to their lack of confidence in being able to provide the same high-level patient care by entering notes and orders electronically. Having mentors guide them helped instill confidence with these systems and the new skill sets. The same physicians who resisted the change from paper to electronic charting now wonder how they provided accurate and efficient care without it.

An example is the use of POCUS (point of care ultrasound). At the start of my practice, central lines, paracentesis, thoracentesis, and lumbar punctures were performed without the guidance of ultrasound unless it was an elective procedure. In those instances, you could schedule a procedure in interventional radiology. Today, in most locations, it is standard of practice to use POCUS for these procedures regardless of urgency.

How did physicians transition their practice to the use of POCUS if they had no formal training? Similarly, how did surgeons learn robotic procedures if not trained in residency? They attended formal courses and likely had a local preceptor or mentors to guide them until they could demonstrate competency to perform the technique independently.

Imposter syndrome describes individuals who don't have the confidence to perform a role when they certainly *do* have the ability. Remember the quote earlier in this book, "Hard work beats talent when talent doesn't work hard"? You **do** have the wherewithal to be great at whatever you put your mind to accomplishing. Imposter syndrome is such a prevalent condition that the next chapter focuses specifically on the topic.

You have existing obligations.

Timing is everything. You may be ready for a change, but factors may tether you to your present role. Perhaps you accepted a scholarship that requires you to pay it back by working in a given environment for several years. Or maybe you're not able to relocate for family reasons. In my case, moving from a clinical physician role to an administrative role would result in a decrease in pay. This prevented me from making a change until our children had completed college.

Circumstances such as caring for a family member, supporting a child's needs, and contributing financially to a household may seem to prohibit making a change today. But take a step back and ask yourself, "Is this a reason to wait, or is it an *excuse* to wait?" Consider whether you can take steps to mitigate these obligations. If there are no workarounds, plan your *next* steps so you are ready to take action immediately upon completion of the obligation. During this waiting period, boost the skills you need to change or advance your career. Take online classes, ask your leadership for a special project to broaden your skill sets, and ask to be mentored.

You're comfortable where you are today — change is overwhelming.

The nature of change is often stressful, and it tends to create more work initially. It's easier *not* to make a change. But you must ask yourself, "What do I value and how important is it to me to advance or change my career?"

A friend of mine began interviewing for a new position after having obtained an MBA. This individual is incredibly smart and has a proven track record. Even so, they were turned down when they applied or they found reasons not to apply for positions in which they were interested. When I spoke with someone who had interviewed this person, I learned that they were very noncommittal during the interview. I asked my friend the tough question: "Are you really ready to make a change?" After a week of thinking about it, the answer was "Not yet."

Consider the television show *Love It or List It*. Homeowners determine that their present home no longer meets their needs. Two professionals come to their rescue. One redesigns their present home to better suit their desires, while the other professional, a realtor, shows them potential new homes they can purchase by selling their older, now-renovated home.

Often, the homes for purchase, frequently new builds, better meet the homeowners' wish list than their newly remodeled home. At the conclusion of each episode, the homeowners decide if they want to love their present remodeled home or list it in exchange for purchasing a different house. Of 236 episodes, 140 culminated in the homeowners choosing to stay in their present homes. This is a more comfortable choice for most homeowners, as it minimizes change.

You don't have any role models.

There were no female leaders in my department and very few among the 1,200 physicians in the healthcare system where I worked. My request for a mentor was met with laughter because there were no female mentors, and my pursuit of a leadership role was not supported in this culture.

How do you get past this kind of deficiency in your career? For me, it came down to resiliency. I refused to see a closed door. Instead, I saw alternative ways to reach a goal. Your path forward may not be easy, but if you don't push yourself to pursue it, who will? Find a role model if one isn't within your circle. For example, examine the behaviors of people you admire and adopt their behaviors, reach out to someone who has already reached your goals, think about people who inspire you and determine what it is about them that inspires you—and incorporate that into your life.

Your skill sets aren't suitable for the new role.

A lack of skill sets certainly can negatively affect confidence, but let's look at it from a different perspective. If you take a job where you already have all the skills you need, you won't continue to grow and you're likely to get bored. To challenge yourself and continue growing, consider options where you have the potential to perform exceptionally well. All you need is the aptitude to develop a new skill.

When I interview a candidate, they may check many but not all the proficiency boxes on my checklist. If I think they are a good cultural match and have the wherewithal to address their skill deficits, I'll hire that person in a heartbeat over someone who is plug-and-play ready today, as the person with the gaps may far exceed the performance of a plug-and-play employee if given the opportunity.

You don't have enough support to move forward.

You need your cheering squad. You need someone to believe in you. Can you meet your goals without this support? Yes. Will it be easier if you have the support? Yes. When someone believes in you, you believe in yourself.

Perhaps you recall the children's book *The Little Engine That Could,* written by Platt and Monk in the 1930s. This story tells a tale of a train climbing a mountain. The engine pulling this large, heavily loaded train over the mountain breaks. Multiple other engines are asked to pull the train and declined for various reasons, mostly out of concern for failure. Finally, a small steam engine agrees to the task. "I think I can, I think I can" the train's steam engine repeats to itself, often overcoming self-doubt. Through hard work, persistence, and determination, the train overcomes the perceived obstacle of the mountain others were not willing to attempt and achieves its goal.

You are your own steam engine. You can not try out of fear of failure, or you can drive yourself forward with positivity. The choice is yours.

You have a sense of loyalty to your current job/company.

You believe in your organization's ability to execute on its mission. You know you add value to that mission. You ask yourself, "What will happen if I leave?" Maybe you've developed a program and are concerned about its future or the future of your team if you leave. You may feel as if you are abandoning them. While there are exceptions, for the most part, the only one looking out for you is *you*. I will repeat that because it's important that you believe it and understand it: The only one looking out for you is *you*. The void you leave will be filled.

Now, I'm not suggesting that you just pick up and leave — you never want to burn bridges regardless of the situation. Assuming there's a reasonable timeframe for an endpoint, consider waiting until a project is completed. Transitioning your work professionally is important — you want to be respected in terms of how you exit a job.

You like the title but not the job.

Some of you may be in the rut of "climbing the ladder." You start as a staff physician, maybe become the associate chair of a department, followed by the chair, and eventually a dean or chief medical officer. Each rung of the ladder earns greater respect, accountability, and admiration. Stop and think about whether the day-to-day activities of the rungs on the ladder you are climbing excite you.

In this example, I knew I would be leaving my role as medical director of an emergency department. One individual clearly wanted to step into the role following my departure, so I gave him multiple tasks that regularly came under my purview. He did those that he enjoyed but left the less-desirable tasks untouched. I tried providing lists, coaching, being the supportive leader, and being the tough leader, but nothing changed his behavior.

Eventually, I had to have a difficult conversation. I confronted him, pointing out that I'd given him every opportunity to prove that he had the skills to move into the medical director role successfully. He admitted he was only completing the tasks he enjoyed and had no interest in the other aspects of the job. I told him that if he wanted me to recommend him for the promotion, I needed to see him performing every task, whether it was enjoyable or not. He returned one week later, grateful for the conversation. He had recognized that he wanted the title but not the day-to-day functional requirements of the job. It wasn't the right match for him.

You are competing against your spouse/ partner or have family obligations.

This is a tough one, and I am no marriage counselor. The hardest situation is one in which you both want the same job. It's easier if both of you want career advancement but are not in competition with each other. Let's explore some potential circumstances.

At a large association's annual convention, there is a sold-out luncheon for women. Female physicians sit at tables of 10, mentoring each other as we navigate the professional world. I will never forget one woman who worked with her husband in the same hospitalist group. She was asked to apply for the position of associate chief. Her spouse yearned for this position. She was surprised that she was approached rather than her spouse and felt significant guilt. Fortunately, her husband was very supportive. We helped her accept the reality that she was solicited for a reason, she earned the opportunity.

Imagine if that same story included cultural norms in which the man is dominant. That same female physician would not only have to maneuver the delicate relationship with her spouse but also the effects on their immediate and extended families. There's nothing easy about this decision, especially if she desires advancement. She may respect the cultural norms of her family and opt not to take the position.

Changing the channel: My prior CMO was reluctant to hire me into a position that involved a lot of travel because of the potential impact on my family. He could have been reluctant because I would be a female traveling alone. Fortunately, the children were grown, and over our 25+ years of marriage, my husband and I had built a degree of trust and support. My husband saw me more often with this job than when I worked from home as a night shift emergency department physician!

What if there are children involved, you want to start a family, or have other time-consuming obligations? Open and honest communication will lead you to a solution. There was a female in her fifth year of surgical residency applying for a fellowship in cardiothoracic surgery whom I admired as a medical student. Her spouse was a non-physician professional. For them, a live-in nanny was the answer. My husband and I wanted to raise our children ourselves. Daycare and grandparents were the answer for us until the kids entered preschool; then, my husband had the opportunity to be a stay-at-home dad.

One more scenario to contemplate: You choose to slow down in your career for a time to be a stay-at-home parent. You may work part-time or even full-time but not taking on added responsibilities. What impacts will this have on your career trajectory, assuming you want to advance your leadership options?

Although I agree with the idea that being a stay-at-home parent or a part-time stay-at-home parent should not harm the possibility of future advancement, I am more of a realist. Organizations cannot wait for you to be ready. As others gain more leadership experience while you opt for a better work-life balance, they will continue to progress up the leadership ranks. This does not preclude you from advancing when you are free from constraints; however, it may place you on a lower rung of the ladder than you otherwise might be. This is my story, and in retrospect, I would not change the decisions we made as a family.

No decision is permanent. If you feel you made a choice that does not meet the situational needs, you can change that path without judgment or regret.

You are restricted for one reason or another.

I personally do not accept a closed door as a reason not to proceed. On the contrary, I find a closed door exhilarating, as I can investigate other options as workarounds to solve a problem.

Let's use the example of being unable to relocate because you are the only family member in close proximity to help care for an elderly family member. Let's say it is your mom. Mom lives alone, but you have concerns for her safety in her current living situation. You visit about once a week to deliver groceries and other necessities, in addition to visiting her for an hour. You speak with her on the phone daily. In your heart and mind, you could not begin to contemplate moving out of the area.

This door is closed until the situation changes. Bear in mind, there are options that could meet your needs as well as your mom's. For example, an independent living facility has some benefits. Meals are provided, or mom can still cook for herself. Van service will take her to stores, the movies, and other activities. Mom's social isolation decreases. She has more energy and enthusiasm. You teach her how to FaceTime. Your mom's only regret is that she did not move to this facility sooner!

Reassured that mom is in a great place, you sell her home and relocate to begin your new opportunity. You FaceTime with mom a few times a week. You visit her once a month, spending more dedicated time with her than you did when you lived in the same town. Your closed-door situation has become a win-win for all!

You have experienced "arrival fallacy" in the past.

Arrival fallacy is when you set an expectation that achieving a given goal will bring you happiness and fulfillment; however, when you reach the destination, it does not deliver those results. Imagine deciding to step out of the academic arena into a highly reputable private practice that offers a significantly higher salary and greater autonomy. You are filled with excitement. Shortly after making the transition, you find you are working longer hours and taking more weekend call than in your previous position. You are making 1.5 times your prior salary. You do not feel fulfilled. The increased cash flow has not created the happiness for which you yearned, and your work-life balance has not improved. This situation will bias you to future decisions, especially if you have experienced recurrent arrival fallacy in the past.

The same concept can be applied to buying a home. You decide to move out of an apartment in the city to a more rural setting. Greater privacy, more space, no homeowner's association rules, and fresh air await you. You soon learn the continual upkeep of the home is greater than imagined. Instead of lounging poolside in the privacy of your own home, you are buying pool chemicals, fishing leaves out of the pool, trimming trees, and mowing the lawn rather than relaxing. The options of nearby restaurants do not meet your expectations. And you no longer have a doorman (or woman) to accept your packages and dry cleaning. This change is a definite adjustment. You love your home but the lack of local amenities and the longer commute to work make you realize that this home did not deliver the joy you anticipated.

You have not clarified your personal values.

There are no right or wrong values, as long as you respect others. When you look at a menu, you immediately dismiss some options while placing others high on your list of what you may order. The same is true with values. None is right or wrong. Values are a preference. It is important to narrow down your list of the values that are most important to you. I recommend three to five values.

Defining your personal values does not, on the surface, appear difficult. Yet, many people do not take the time to clearly define their own personal values. Here is a list of 50 personal values to consider. I am sure you can add some to this list.

1. **Curiosity**: That innate desire to explore the unknown, ask meaningful questions, and continuously learn about the world around you.
2. **Accountability**: Taking full ownership of your actions and circumstances, including acknowledging mistakes and committing to your objectives.
3. **Family**: Prioritizing meaningful relationships with loved ones and dedicating quality time to nurture those bonds.
4. **Innovation**: Embracing creative problem-solving and having the courage to challenge conventional thinking with novel approaches.
5. **Self-compassion**: Treating yourself with kindness and understanding, recognizing that you're doing your best rather than being overly self-critical.
6. **Respect**: Showing genuine appreciation and consideration for others, honoring what makes each individual special.

7. **Courage:** Acting despite fear or uncertainty, understanding that bravery manifests differently for everyone.
8. **Flexibility:** Demonstrating mental agility by adapting your thinking and smoothly handling unexpected changes or assignments.
9. **Empowerment:** Inspiring others to recognize their capabilities and supporting them as they reach their full potential.
10. **Gratitude:** Recognizing and appreciating the positive aspects of your life, often through daily reflection practices.
11. **Loyalty:** Standing by others consistently through both good times and challenging periods, whether in friendships, relationships, or professional settings.
12. **Assertiveness:** Expressing yourself with confidence and conviction, advocating for your needs in a direct yet respectful manner.
13. **Independence:** Embracing self-sufficiency and preferring to accomplish tasks on your own while remaining open to collaboration when needed.
14. **Wellness:** Prioritizing your physical and mental health through consistent healthy habits that support long-term vitality.
15. **Hard work:** Committing maximum effort to your endeavors and maintaining dedication even when facing difficulties.
16. **Community:** Fostering a sense of belonging and connection within groups, recognizing the mental health benefits of being part of something larger.
17. **Collaboration:** Working effectively with others to achieve shared goals and bringing out everyone's best contributions.
18. **Generosity:** Freely giving your resources — whether time, kindness, attention, or material goods — to benefit others.
19. **Forgiveness:** Releasing resentment and painful memories rather than allowing them to cause ongoing harm.
20. **Adaptability:** Maintaining resilience when facing obstacles or uncomfortable emotions, flowing with circumstances rather than resisting them.

21. **Self-improvement:** Continuously seeking opportunities for personal development through dedicated effort and clear goal-setting.
22. **Authenticity:** Staying true to yourself regardless of others' judgments, refusing to pretend or compromise your genuine identity.
23. **Purpose:** Making intentional choices that reflect your deepest values and living with clear direction.
24. **Open-mindedness:** Welcoming different viewpoints and experiences, showing enthusiasm for meeting diverse people and understanding varied cultures.
25. **Frugality:** Managing finances wisely through careful spending habits and thoughtful resource allocation.
26. **Joy:** Discovering delight in everyday moments and allowing positive energy to radiate from within.
27. **Honesty:** Speaking truthfully with both courage and sensitivity, balancing directness with empathy.
28. **Education:** Cherishing the lifelong journey of acquiring knowledge and embracing learning opportunities at every stage.
29. **Connection:** Building authentic relationships where people feel genuinely valued and understood.
30. **Reliability:** Consistently following through on commitments and being someone others can count on without question.
31. **Balance:** Maintaining healthy equilibrium across all life areas, preventing any single aspect from dominating your time and energy.
32. **Perseverance:** Demonstrating resilience and determination to continue moving forward despite setbacks and challenges.
33. **Giving support:** Offering a compassionate presence and listening ear when others navigate difficult life circumstances.
34. **Humility:** Remaining grounded and authentic regardless of achievements or status.
35. **Equity:** Ensuring everyone receives the specific resources and opportunities they need to thrive, recognizing that fairness doesn't mean identical treatment.

36. **Creativity:** Harnessing imagination for expression and innovation, whether through arts, problem-solving, or other inventive pursuits.

37. **Justice:** Advocating for fairness and working to ensure everyone receives equal treatment and opportunities.

38. **Altruism:** Acting selflessly for the collective benefit, helping others without expectation of personal gain.

39. **Self-reflection:** Valuing introspection and self-awareness, engaging in thoughtful examination of your thoughts and actions.

40. **Optimism:** Maintaining hope and finding positive possibilities even during challenging circumstances.

41. **Self-respect:** Honoring your own worth and refusing to accept mistreatment, including establishing healthy boundaries when necessary.

42. **Patience:** Remaining calm during delays or frustrations, trusting that worthwhile outcomes require time.

43. **Personal growth:** Striving to evolve beyond your previous self across emotional, physical, or intellectual dimensions.

44. **Sustainability:** Taking responsibility for environmental impact through conscious choices that protect the planet and its inhabitants.

45. **Discipline:** Maintaining commitment to necessary tasks and responsibilities even when distractions or easier options beckon.

46. **Dependability:** Being a consistent presence that others can trust to meet expectations and obligations.

47. **Ambition:** Cultivating internal motivation that drives you toward aspirations and personal excellence.

48. **Uniqueness:** Celebrating individuality and embracing what sets you apart, comfortable with nonconformity.

49. **Integrity:** Consistently choosing ethical actions regardless of who's observing, maintaining honesty even in private moments.

50. **Well-being:** Cultivating overall happiness and health, recognizing that chronic stress diminishes quality of life and requires proactive self-care.

One value that is not included in this top 50 list deserves further attention: financial wealth. As physicians, we dedicate our lives to helping others. Can the values of altruism and wealth be combined? Absolutely, by creating a balance. A medical student who is considering residency programs and places a high value on wealth may be more likely to choose orthopedics, plastic surgery, or cardiology than endocrinology or pediatrics because the former are the three highest-compensated specialties. Physicians in these top-paying specialties are not necessarily in these fields solely because of the money. They may have the skills and the interest to succeed in these areas, as well as the interest in maintaining a certain lifestyle. There's nothing wrong with that.

If you are getting ready to sign a contract, explore opportunities to earn additional dollars on top of your expected job responsibilities, which may include additional pay for high work product generating greater RVUs, the ability to moonlight, or perhaps working additional shifts. The times will change, so working additional shifts may be an option today while the department is short-staffed.

Your values can and will change over time, especially as you transition from early- to mid- to late-stage career. You may value wealth, diving into work 24/7 until you have a family or reach a point of burnout. At that point, you may not value money as much as work-life balance. At this juncture in your career, general cardiology may be the perfect match for your values.

You should always stay true to your values. A work environment that stifles your ability to live your values has a very high likelihood of creating job dissatisfaction. Today, I am very mission-driven. I must believe in what I do every day as a driver to engage myself fully with my work. I do enjoy financial wealth; however, I am willing to sacrifice a portion of my compensation to choose a company where I am better aligned with the mission. Guiding your career decision-making tree should be your personal top-rated core values.

Putting It Together

Make an exhaustive list of risks and benefits for any future decisions. Speak with others who have experience in similar situations.

Will the change you are contemplating meet your needs or add to your frustrations? The grass is not always greener on the other side, despite perceptions.

This chapter unveils several factors that may be holding you back. After objectively and honestly analyzing your situation, develop a personalized action plan tailored to your specific needs. I cannot stress enough the importance of being honest with yourself. Your decision may be to not make a change as you recognize you are where you want to be in your career. Not making a change may involve an action plan of thoughtful discussion with others who may be pushing you for change. You may need to delay making a change due to several variables. This delay could represent an unrecognized opportunity to gain much-needed skills or experience. You determine you are now fully engaged and motivated to take that next step. Regardless of the endpoint following this reflection, your plan will be your own, individualized from all others.

Take a step back and be honest with yourself. Do you really want to make a change? If you do, is something nevertheless holding you back?

In the words of Coco Chanel, "Success is most often achieved by those who don't know that failure is inevitable."

IN SUMMARY:

1. If you have decided to make a change without moving ahead with your plan, you may have some subconscious factors holding you back.
2. Frequently unrecognized emotions drive your decision-making process.
3. You must be honest with yourself, recognizing and evaluating all factors influencing your thought process.
4. I repeat, you must be honest with yourself, taking the time to understand your choices and emotions.
5. Defining your top values helps to guide your career choices, leading to higher job satisfaction.
6. After weighing these drivers, establish your action plan, which may or may not include a career change.

Imposter Syndrome

CONFIDENCE

im·pos·tor syn·drome

noun: "The persistent inability to believe that one's success is deserved or has been legitimately achieved as a result of one's own efforts or skills."

Think of a time in your life when you were asked to lead a project or to present in front of an audience. Did you ever wonder, "Why did they choose me? Will they realize that I don't have the skills they may think I have?" Did this situation provoke anxiety or fear? Did you believe that someone else was better suited for the task? What if you didn't have the solution? What if you were asked a question you couldn't answer? What would they think of you if you did not live up to their expectations?

If you relate to any of the above, you are not alone. I witnessed plenty of cases of imposter syndrome when I was teaching an online physician leadership class for a large association. My role was to post thought-provoking questions on leadership experiences related to change management following didactic lectures by various speakers. The students' grades were dependent on their responses to a percentage of the posted questions. I posted an out-of-the-box question that started with a story about my own insecurities and imposter syndrome, and then I asked them to give examples if they'd ever felt the same way. The question was totally unrelated to the lecture.

I was surprised that every student responded to this question year after year — my usual response rate was 50%. Not only did they respond with their own stories, but they also expressed relief that they weren't alone with these thoughts and experiences. The community unified behind each person, empathizing with their responses.

Impostor syndrome was never discussed during any of my medical school, residency, MBA, leadership, or other educational trainings! Why not?

I believe that the topic is somewhat analogous to speaking about mental health disorders — after all, there are negative connotations associated with feeling insecure. Why would you be promoted if you doubted that you had the requisite skills to succeed? Why should someone believe in you if you don't believe in yourself? A more significant question is, why do so many highly educated and skilled individuals lack confidence in themselves?

Imposter syndrome was initially identified as a trait displayed by women, but in my experience, anyone who differs from the "norm" of a given work culture — man or woman— is more likely to experience imposter syndrome. In my own case, I was not a tall white male, which used to be the predominant "look" of hospital leadership. Consider other examples: a female participating in a predominantly male board meeting, a physician whose primary language is not English but who is involved in an American residency program, a physician who wears their native dress. In all these scenarios, it can be difficult to find a role model or someone with whom you can identify.

Unconscious bias often prohibits you from being the first choice for a promotion or an opportunity. This situation likewise makes you question your self-worth. "Was I too ambitious with my goals?" "What made me think I could do that job?" Your self-doubt cripples you into not applying for the next role, even though you're quite capable of performing it well. Your doubt becomes a self-fulfilling prophecy that you are not "good enough." Meanwhile, others with a fraction of your skill sets are advancing their careers right in front of your eyes.

During one of my leadership development presentations recently, an attendee eloquently described how she questioned herself every time she received accolades at work. One incident she recalled vividly was the positive comments others expressed after she delivered a talk to the group. "Did they feel sorry for me because I moved to the United States alone and speak little English?" she wondered.

"Are they just being kind? Did I really deserve those accolades? Did they say that to me because it was politically correct to tell me I did something well? Do they usually view me as substandard, and today I did a better job?"

During a panel discussion about imposter syndrome, participants shared the following scenario. Two physicians in residency performed poorly on Part 2 of the boards. One resident was called into a meeting by her adviser and asked if medicine was the right career path for her. If she could not pass Part 2 of the board exam, the adviser said, she may not have a career in clinical medicine. The other resident was called into a meeting with her adviser and told, "We have a problem to solve. Let's come up with a plan to get you over this hurdle." Same performance on the board exam, but two different responses: one with negative connotations and one with a positive plan. Which resident was beaten down and which resident believed she would succeed? Who left their meeting feeling disgraced and a failure? Who left the meeting feeling supported and worthy of being a physician? Unquestionably, the resident with the negative response to her Part 2 board exam outcome is more likely to lack confidence as she moves forward in her career as a physician and, thus, more likely to suffer from impostor syndrome.

For most of my life, I couldn't say "Thank you" without adding a "but" such as, "Thank you, *but* it was because I was in the right place at the right time." I felt very justified in adding the "but" until the day a small group of us were performing an executive coaching session for a colleague. We made it clear that our coaching and feedback were not just for him — it was a two-way street with all who were participating. This colleague informed me that I added the "but" after he thanked me for something, it made him feel as though I didn't value his "Job well done!" comments. A light bulb went off in my head. I still catch myself adding the "but" more often than I'd like.

In July 2024, Korn Ferry published the results of a survey that included responses from more than 10,000 professionals at all levels, from entry to CEO, across six countries. According to the Workforce 2024 Global Insights Report, an astonishing 71% of CEOs reported experiencing imposter syndrome, versus 65% of senior executives and 33% in the early-stage professional group. Eighty-five percent of the same CEOs surveyed believed they were competent in their role.

True imposter syndrome has many negative impacts on your career. Your belief that you're not qualified becomes a self-fulfilling prophecy. You don't apply for positions even though you're quite capable of excelling in the role. You don't move into areas that might make you feel uncomfortable as you grow and develop your skill sets. You believe someone else will do a better job. You are afraid of failing because you lack the necessary skills to succeed. But none of this makes sense. Leaders are not born with the skills they need to lead; they develop their competencies over time, often stepping into new territories where they had to learn new skills to succeed. For years, I was told that I couldn't advance in my career from being a physician in the emergency department to becoming someone with leadership responsibilities because I was residency-trained in internal medicine and not emergency medicine. Therefore, I was surprised when I was asked to be the medical director for an emergency department. Even though I wanted the leadership role, my initial response was that I wasn't the best choice to fill the need because I wasn't residency-trained in emergency medicine — despite being a medical director at an urgent care company at the time.

The person who offered me the position took the time to explore why I believed I wasn't the correct fit. He explained to me, "I want someone who's a great leader and not the best-trained emergency department physician." He recognized how to fit the puzzle pieces together to ensure a well-functioning emergency department, and in doing so, he opened the door, and I stepped through it. It was the next rung of my leadership climb.

I was once asked in an interview if I had ever moved past impostor syndrome. I was able to confidently answer that yes, I had. How do you move past this kind of deep self-doubt? For me, at least, resilience kept me going. I was going to find a way to be successful! Even if someone closed a door, I would find a side door or a back door to open. **Success does not equate to confidence. Confidence does not equate to competence.**

36

Just because someone projects confidence doesn't mean they feel confident internally. Competence is gained through experience, and people must be given opportunities to acquire it. If you experience imposter syndrome, what can you do to combat the emotions? First, recognize you are not alone. Consider a mentor, professional coach, or trusted acquaintance who will not provide you with answers but will guide you in developing confidence in your decision-making and other skill sets. Many CEOs or high-level executives reach out to peers with equal experience for guidance as they navigate the trajectory of a company. The higher your level of leadership, the narrower your pool of individuals to confide in.

As physicians, it's in our nature to help others. Speak openly about your experiences so that others won't feel isolated. Be the role model you wish you'd had or the one who helped you gain confidence and afforded you the chance to grow your skills and competencies. Provide opportunities for others. I'm hopeful the times are changing more toward inclusivity! Nowadays, the field has many young physicians who may differ from you in one way or another. I challenge you to be that positive mentor guiding others through these hidden fears and self-doubt.

The following poem was written by Dr. Priya Radhakrishnan, the chief academic officer for HonorHealth, medical director of HonorHealth Employee Health, and a clinical professor of medicine at the University of Arizona College of Medicine-Phoenix. She is completing her term as chair of the Board of Governors for the American College of Physicians. She shared this powerful poem at a leadership session for early-career physicians exploring imposter syndrome.

THE ACCENT

She stepped into a Starbucks
Her thirst was strong
She stood in line
Timid was she for this was a first

All she desired was a taste of home

Where they called it 'expresso'
At the corner cafe
Frothy milk with a touch of coffee
With an almond biscuit
Was manna from Heaven

She walked the streets of New York
With five dollars for the day
She stopped at Starbucks
Pressed her nose to the door
Sat outside till the crowd thinned

Then she sauntered in from the cold
Stylish she thought she was
Little did she know
That others saw her as gauche

Suddenly swarms of people did come
She stood in line
All she wanted was her 'expresso'
When her turn came
She stammered her order
Burnt by the scorn that Barista added to her order

When she got her coffee
It was black and dark
Bitter as the humiliation she felt
There was no trace of the milky frothy goodness of her childhood
drink

For in America her 'expresso'
Was a cappuccino
An almond biscuit there was none
Her language was foreign
Her accent too thick

She sipped her coffee
She was naive
She was sad

The bitterness of the coffee
Penetrated her core
Unable to stomach it
She threw it in the trash
Along with her dreams

Years went by
She loved to grow her new land
Starbucks was a given
Jokes she would share
The baristas knew her by name And her drink
For a double espresso was her fave
She had arrived accent and all

IN SUMMARY:

1. Imposter syndrome is more commonplace than previously recognized.
2. At some point in your career, you are more likely than not to experience some degree of imposter syndrome.
3. Imposter syndrome can negatively impact your career trajectory.
4. Understanding how to cope with the feelings of imposter syndrome will minimize the negative impacts.
5. Do not feel isolated from imposter syndrome. You are far from alone.

Greatest Strength Equals Greatest Weakness

BALANCE

Many years ago, someone told me that a person's greatest strength is also their greatest weakness. Let me share a story.

Dr. Jane Doe has an entrepreneurial spirit. She is very high-energy and gets bored easily. She launches multiple businesses. Each business has the potential to succeed on its own. Dr. Doe spreads her focus in many directions, launching each business. She does not focus on the success of one business before launching the next one. None of the entities is profitable, and she eventually must close each one. Her strength: high energy, causing her to get bored easily, yields a great entrepreneurial spirit. Her weakness: high energy, causing her to get bored easily, is the downfall of her business lines.

Personality Profiles

There are many personality profile evaluations to choose from; however, I will use the DiSC tool for simplicity. If you are not familiar with the DiSC personality profile, it is an assessment that takes about 15 minutes to complete. You get a score in each of four categories. Your highest-scoring categories define your personality in simplistic terms.

- D = dominance: Direct, results-oriented, firm, strong-willed, and forceful.
- I = influence: Outgoing, enthusiastic, optimistic, high-spirited, and lively.
- S = steadiness: Even-tempered, accommodating, patient, humble, and tactful.
- C = conscientious: Analytical, reserved, precise, private, and systematic.

If your two strongest categories are D and C, you are designated as a DC and are task-oriented. CS individuals are reserved while DI's are outgoing. If you are an IS, you are people-oriented.

Why is it important to identify a personality type? These designations provide insight into a person's strengths, what motivates them, the best forms of communication, and how to approach conflict resolution and productivity. Many CEOs are D predominant. Scientists have a high prevalence of C personalities. An I personality wants to be rewarded with a celebration for a job well done, while a C may appreciate some additional PTO as their recognition.

The DiSC helps you better understand your team, but how does it help you as an individual? First, let's briefly comment on how to use personality types in leadership. If you are a D and enter a meeting with a group of S individuals, they may provide the input you seek because they are accommodating. Will their input be useful if they are sharing only what they perceive you want to hear? They may believe you do not value the input of others when that is far from the truth! If you are a C person who needs data and time to digest data, a D personality can be exhausting because they are assertive, persistent, and competitive. An S personality can perceive a D personality as abrasive at times. You can find more about the DiSC personalities at https://www.discprofile.com.

The MBTI® (Myers-Briggs) personality profile is another common, easy-to-access, scientifically proven personality profile assessment. It takes about 45 minutes to complete. The following information on MBTI is directly from the website (https://www.mbtionline.com). The assessment looks at four different areas, assigning one of two personality traits to each of the four categories, yielding 16 possible combinations. The letters indicate personality preferences in four key areas:

- How you get your energy (E–I: Extraversion vs. Introversion).
- How you take in information and learn (S–N: Sensing vs. Intuition).
- How you make decisions (T–F: Thinking vs. Feeling).
- How you like to organize your time and environment (J–P: Judging vs. Perceiving).

One letter from each category is combined to identify a four-letter personality preference, such as ISTJ, which happens to be the most common pairing of the 16 types found in the global population. As an illustrative example, the following is a brief outline of the ISTJ personality:

- Rely on past experiences when making decisions.
- Decisive, focused, and efficient; interested in absorbing information that will improve their work.
- Like strengthening their current relationships rather than seeking new ones.
- Tend to "play the hits" in their lives, finding joy and comfort in the things they know they like.

ISTJ Strengths:

- Dependable, straightforward, and logical.
- Like to work with clear processes, tend to stick with what works, and usually learn from their mistakes.
- Rely on facts and figures so they can do their best at any given task.
- Like to have clear, step-by-step instructions for exactly what needs to be done so they can complete a job properly the first time.
- Like to develop strong, loyal bonds with the people in their lives and tend to be traditional in their desire for a strong family unit.

ISTJ Opportunities for Development:

- Value structure and logic; they can appear rigid in their approach to the world.
- Can become irritated or stressed if unforeseen circumstances challenge their approach.
- May be overly critical of people who have different ideas or ways of doing things.
- Because they tend to focus more on tasks than interpersonal relationships, they can be perceived as impersonal.

ISTJ Work Preferences:

- Tend to appreciate jobs with structure, routine, and dependability.
- Don't particularly crave excitement or change in the workplace. Instead, they like to learn all there is to know about their job and are often adept at absorbing and retaining this information.
- Consider becoming an expert in their field a measure of success.
- Enjoy a good balance of teamwork and privacy in the workplace, so they don't typically favor novelty office spaces.
- Appreciate the reliability that certain career paths afford—such as the steady pay, the benefits, and the potential for advancement.

ISTJ Leadership Style:

- Absorb information from their own experiences. They tend to take note of what worked well or didn't work in the past, then apply these lessons to managing a team or running a business.
- Tend to be kind and considerate without being too personal yet might appear rigid under stress.

ISTJs on a Team:

- Good team players, provided they know their role and what is expected of them. They prefer clear, concise instructions and direct communication between team members.
- Main priority is to get the job done well.
- While they appreciate the social elements of teamwork, they dislike too much small talk. They tend to be hard on others it they suspect them of slacking or not pulling their weight.

ISTJs and Conflict:

- See conflict as part of life. Rather than spending a lot of time discussing their feelings, they usually attempt to resolve a conflict as soon as possible so that both parties can move on with their lives.

If you take the MBTI, you will be provided with in-depth information on the 16 different profiles, helping you better understand yourself and others.

Some personalities are better suited for some roles than others; however, any of these personalities can succeed in any role. You just need the emotional intelligence to understand your strengths, how you are perceived, where you may excel, and what may bring you greater personal satisfaction. An analytical personality may become frustrated with someone who expresses unconventional thinking. A dominant personality will become impatient reading a long email or engaging in an extended discussion. An influencer can be so energetic and lively that they are not taken seriously.

The same concepts can be applied to your career choice. As a group, physicians are smart, dynamic individuals. We can adapt to many situations. We may change our approach for a patient who is very analytical and wants every detail of an illness prior to discussing treatment options, versus a patient who states, "You are the doctor. You tell me what to do."

A general radiologist is likely to have a different personality from an emergency department physician. The general radiologist reads one film at a time systematically analyzing each study. Interactions, for non-interventional radiologists, are mostly limited to peers and team members. The emergency room physician is multitasking patient care to the highest degree, performing bedside care and procedures, interacting with team members, patients, families, and visitors every second of their shift, not knowing when the organized chaos will be interrupted by an "emergency." Some people thrive in the organized chaos situation, while others would prefer to be hit by a truck.

Psychometric Testing

Psychometric testing is a more comprehensive assessment beyond personality testing, providing more in-depth insights into a person's cognitive abilities and character. It includes a personality test supplemented by situational judgement tests (SJTs) and aptitude tests. This evaluation often includes a Likert scale (a rating from 1 to 5 representing strongly disagree to strongly agree), opening the door for *social desirability bias* impacting the results. During the assessment, individuals often record what they perceive to be the best answer rather than answering honestly. Candid responses yield the best results. Other portions evaluate abstract, deductive, inductive, numerical, and verbal reasoning. The STJs section often involves a multiple-choice response.

Psychometric testing is a commonly utilized tool in the hiring process as a supplement to the interview, which can be deceiving. Candidates can interview well but not perform well. I was nervous when a large executive recruiting firm invited me to complete psychometric testing as a routine piece of their intake process. I apprehensively opened the results, concerned that my emotional EQ could be significantly deviated from the results in front of me. I breathed a great sigh of relief that my results reinforced my goals. I share these results with potential employers for a win-win outcome.

Consider engaging in psychometric testing to gain insights into your own personality and abilities. You will gain eye-opening, accurate perceptions of yourself. Utilize this information to align your career choices with your traits.

Personal Brand

Personality profiles extend into your personal brand — how others view you. How others view you can be colored by your actions — intended and unintended. When you are stressed or tired, you may revert to your strongest personality traits to cope with the stressful situation. If that trait shows you in a negative light, you've damaged your personal brand. You can be intentional in your actions to raise your brand. Developing your personal brand should be an intentional, 24/7 activity. Maya Angelou's famous quote "I've learned that people will forget what you said, people will forget what you did, but they will never forget how you made them feel" embodies a personal brand. What do you want your personal brand to reflect? Is it trust? Consistency? Friendship? Dependability? Reflect on some of your finest moments. Contrast these moments with times you felt stressed or tired. Did your personal brand deviate when you were under stress?

You may have different personal brands: one at work, one as a parent, one as a spouse, etc. There is likely considerable overlap, as that is your personality regardless of the situation. Consistency with each of your personal brands must be deliberate.

Strongly consider taking a personality profile test. Use the results to improve your emotional intelligence. Contemplate how your results may align with various career path choices. These results can be applied to many life circumstances, but in the context of our discussions, indulge in exploring your desires and how they match up to your dream job. What is your greatest strength? How does your greatest strength translate into your greatest weakness?

IN SUMMARY:

1. Understanding your emotional intelligence is critical for success.
2. Applying your emotional intelligence yields effective leadership through influence, effective communication, and striking chords to have team members perceive they are genuinely valued.
3. Understanding your personality profile can help guide your career path decision by aligning your traits to well-suited positions for both positive objective and emotional outcomes.
4. Psychometric testing is gaining momentum in the hiring process. It is a valuable assessment in your career path journey for key decision-making determinations.

Mentorship and Coaching

ANGELS

I conceptualize mentors as angels sitting on your shoulder. They are there when you need them. They guide you on your leadership journey. They are honest and facilitate you being the best you. They volunteer at no financial cost to you. Sounds like a perfect addition to your tool kit. Many wish it were that easy.

First, let's set straight any confusion about the difference between preceptors, mentors, and professional leadership coaches:

Preceptor: A preceptor is an experienced practitioner who provides supervision during clinical practice and facilitates the application of theory to practice for students and staff learners (from *Merriam-Webster Dictionary*).

Mentor: A mentor is a professional, working alliance in which individuals work together over time to support the personal and professional growth, development, and success of the relational partners through the provision of career and psychosocial support (from the NIH website).

Coach: Workplace coaching typically involves a series of one-on-one conversations between the coach and the coachee. The coach provides feedback, guidance, and support to help the coachee set goals, identify obstacles, and create action plans. (from *Britannica Dictionary*).

Preceptors

Preceptors instruct learners who need to acquire skills about which the preceptor has expertise. You likely had preceptors during residency. They may be upper-level residents teaching you the art of clinical patient care. They may teach you clinical procedures. Other examples include attendings precepting patient care rounds or surgical techniques. New employees frequently have preceptors during the onboarding period, ensuring understanding of the workplace expectations, culture, and workflows. The phase spent with a preceptor is usually time-limited. Once a preceptor's task is completed with the preceptee, the formal relationship concludes.

Think of times you have interacted with preceptors. I suspect the high-performing preceptors made you feel valued. No question was too small or too big. They reached out to you, offering support without being prompted. They were not distracted when interacting with you, as you were their prime focus at that moment. You felt comfortable approaching them with questions. They made you feel confident.

A common error of anyone who is teaching another is to educate them in a way that best matches your own learning style. Some preceptees learn best by watching and others by doing. Some jump right in while others need time to process what they have learned. Consider a situation when you were learning something new, and it just did not click. Someone else explained it differently to you, and instantly the concept became clear and understandable. This does not only apply to medicine. Try precepting an elementary school student through different math problems!

It is often said, "Always treat others as you would like to be treated." The next time you are in a precepting role, I challenge you to think about how your interaction will impact a preceptee. An obstetrician expressed this concept to me when I was a medical student, explaining that they deliver hundreds upon hundreds of infants in their career, and most are not memorable to the obstetrician. On the other hand, the mom and those surrounding her in the room will always remember their delivery experience, including the comments and actions of the obstetrician. Make the interaction the best experience of their life.

Sometimes it may be hard to put your best foot forward as a preceptor. You are preoccupied with competing priorities. Maybe you never volunteered to be a preceptor, as precepting is not your passion. You may ask yourself, "What's in it for me?" The answer is a great deal. Consider the following scenario:

You are a medical director and have a new employee named Dr. John Doe. You have many meetings scheduled, plus your own small patient panel. You need to submit your budget requests by the end of the week. You are the only person available to precept Dr. Doe through his orientation. Dr. Doe appears to catch on quickly. You take the path of trying to expedite precepting this person through orientation and send him out on his own to learn the rest. You respectfully mention everything you have on your plate, assuring Dr. Doe that he can call you anytime with questions. Dr. Doe wants to please you. He tells you he understands, and he will reach out if he needs help, thus freeing you up to tend to other tasks.

A few weeks later, you start to hear rumblings and maybe a few complaints about Dr. Doe. He is not showing up at multidisciplinary rounds. Notes are not completed in a timely fashion. His sign-outs are not as expected. The staff and other physicians on the team have started developing negative perceptions about Dr. Doe. He is just not the good fit you thought he would be when you hired him. You are still busy and delay having a conversation with Dr. Doe, as nothing overwhelmingly serious has been brought to your attention.

At Dr. Doe's 90-day review, you discuss some of the concerns shared with you. Dr. Doe expresses that he was unaware that attendance at multidisciplinary rounds is mandatory. He says that at his last job, he was asked to attend multidisciplinary rounds only when needed, and he assumed it was the same here. As for not completing medical records on time, his previous job required chart completion within 7 days. He likes to be thorough, so he works on his charts at home during his days off. During his orientation with you, he was not made aware that chart completion is required within 72 hours at this facility. You review his charts, and not only are they well documented, but he generates high RVUs. Verbal sign-outs were his routine at his past facility, and he was not introduced to the electronic sign-outs at this facility.

51

You feel better recognizing that Dr. Doe is a good doctor who was unaware of certain expectations that should have been covered during his orientation, and which are now clear. Dr. Doe expressed his appreciation for your clarifying the expectations. Dr. Doe is very conscientious, and you both are confident these behaviors will change. On the other hand, Dr. Doe leaves the meeting feeling he is not doing a satisfactory job. He has always been a high performer. He feels he let you down, but acknowledges, to himself, he could not abide by rules that were never shared with him.

Over the ensuing weeks, Dr. Doe notices that the other physicians on his team and staff do not respond positively to him. Dr. Doe chooses to leave your team and finds employment at a competitor. Physicians at the competitor, who are considering applying for a job on your team, ask Dr. Doe about his experience and why he elected to leave. You now have the high financial cost of recruiting another physician, the negative impact on your team's culture from being short-staffed, and a negative impact on patient quality of care, with the present team of physicians having less time to spend with each patient.

Taking this a step further, let's fast forward 15 years. You are applying for a regional medical director position with a cutting-edge company. The CMO is Dr. Doe. You have equal qualifications to other applicants. Who is Dr. Doe more likely to hire?

Now consider the path you could have taken as a preceptor. You dedicate the time and attention to precepting Dr. Doe during his orientation. You have a few late nights burrowing through your pile of work. Dr. Doe rapidly propels to one of the top-performing physicians on your team. There is a positive impact on culture. It would not be unusual for Dr. Doe, under your mentorship, to advance to higher-level leadership roles. He may seek you out to be on his team when he becomes the CMO of the cutting-edge company.

How do you want to be remembered as a preceptor?

Mentors

I acknowledge two of my mentors on the dedication page of this book: Michael Ammazzalorso (posthumously) and Michael Le.

You have likely already experienced preceptors and are now a preceptor yourself. Your career advancement or change will be hard to navigate without a mentor. Mentors are not standing on a street corner waiting for the opportunity to be chosen as a mentor. So how does one go about engaging with a mentor?

First, ask yourself what you want to get out of the relationship. A mentor does not have a magic wand that lands you in a dream job filled with happiness, fame, and fortune. You need to identify your goals of being mentored. It is difficult for a mentor to provide value if you do not identify these needs. Here are some examples:

- You are the vice chair of a department. You need to turn around some disruptive behaviors of team members. You may request mentoring from the director of people management (human resources)on having difficult conversations, as you view these discussions as confrontational, which is not your personality at all!
- You may have received feedback on your last performance review outlining examples of when you have not been perceived as having a collaborative approach. You are looking for a mentor to help you recognize what behaviors are being perceived as noncollaborative and how to approach situations differently.
- You want to start a hospital-at-home program to support a value-based care contract. The hospital administration is willing to consider your proposal. They are requesting you return with a business plan. You don't know where to begin putting together a business plan.
- Your healthcare system just acquired a new hospital. You are charged with integrating the Department of Surgery between the two hospitals. You recognize that if this is not done correctly, multiple surgeons may leave the institution. You are seeking mentorship on how to achieve this goal effectively.

Outlining clear goals will guide you to the best mentor. In the examples above, you would not ask the director of people management to help you write a business plan, nor would you ask the CFO to guide you in having difficult conversations.

Determining the target skill(s) you want to gain from the mentorship involves writing one or more SMART goals. Documenting goals in this format greatly increases your likelihood of attaining the desired outcome. The following outlines the components of a SMART goal:

- **Specific: What exactly do you want to accomplish?**
- **Measurable: You must be able to objectively measure the goals.**
- **Attainable: They must be realistic.**
- **Relevant: How is this going to help you?**
- **Time-bound: You must have a specific date or timeline for completion.**

A poorly communicated goal may look something like this: I want to be able to launch a hospital-at-home program with the executive team's approval. In contrast, a well-communicated goal may be expressed as a SMART goal: I want to present a business plan exploring the opportunity to launch a hospital-at-home program, including start-up and long-term financial impacts, to the executive team at the June 4 executive team meeting. Breaking down this example, the specific is "explore the opportunity to launch a hospital-at-home program." The measurable is developing the business plan. This goal is attainable with your mentor's support. This is relevant because you are executing on a value-based care contract and have been asked by the executive team to return with a business plan. Presenting this to the executive team on June 4 completes the time-bound component.

Now that you have identified your mentorship goal(s), you must find the best mentor based on those goals. Mentors are akin to preceptors with respect to what qualities make a good preceptor, although preceptors are often placed in the role, while mentors often volunteer their time in the relationship. A mentor should be open and honest with feedback, safeguarding against going through the motions, and allowing you opportunities to achieve the desired outcomes.

Let's explore this open and honest relationship. This is a two-way street where both the mentor and mentee provide feedback on the progress in meeting the outlined goals. You may need the preceptor to provide you with a better understanding of the process as you develop a business plan for your new hospital-at-home program. You may find yourself feeling defensive with the feedback you receive from the mentor. Before reacting to feedback, it's prudent to explore why you have these internal emotions. Getting feedback, as difficult as it may be to hear, is a gift. I recommend setting expectations surrounding feedback and a safe space for communication about it.

Choosing your direct supervisor as your mentor is a challenging decision. Do you want to expose your weaknesses to the person writing your performance review? Does your supervisor have the best insights to assist you with your given goals? Weigh the risks and benefits if this person becomes your mentor. On the opposite side of the coin, will your supervisor be uncomfortable or anxious if you go to a different source for mentorship? When I was an emergency department physician on the medical board of the hospital, the CEO provided me with mentorship, steering me to a better understanding of the hospital competing priorities for resources. When the chief of emergency services retired, he suggested that the next chief may not have the same level of experience and confidence as he did and may be uncomfortable learning that I had regular access to the CEO. The thought had never crossed my mind that the CEO providing me with mentorship could make my chief uncomfortable as we were not conversing about the emergency department's performance or my chief's performance.

I recommend sharing any mentor relationship within the same institution with your immediate supervisor to avoid any misunderstandings. I was employed at a company that paired mentors with mentees from different departments. It was their practice to share the relationship of any employee engaged in the mentorship program with their immediate supervisor. The details of the private mentorship conversations were not disclosed, only that a mentor-mentee relationship existed.

A word of caution to avoid bias when you make a list of potential mentors. It is human nature to gravitate toward someone who is like you, be it in personality, ethnicity, sexuality, or other characteristics. This is known as affinity or similarity bias. A "similar" person may not have the insights you need, especially if the mentoring involves a behavioral characteristic. The mentor needs to be objective. Friends may have difficulty with feedback objectivity due to concerns about how it will impact the relationship.

Why would someone want to be a mentor, volunteering their time when they already have full plates in front of them? Mentorship is greatly rewarding. The fulfillment of making a positive impact on another physician cannot be overstated. The gratification a mentor feels when a mentee excels is huge. Mentors are continuous learners. They gain from each mentee relationship. Not everyone desires to be a mentor. Personally, I did not have mentors or role models early in my career when I was yearning for one. This is an opportunity for me to give back, ensuring needed support to those who want a mentor with my competencies.

You have identified your mentor and your goals. These goals are accepted or modified by your mentor. Both parties agree to enter a mentor-mentee relationship. You have set the ground rules. The next step is to place regular meetings on your calendars. The scheduled meetings ensure forward progress continues. Both you and your mentor are busy. Life will frequently get in the way unless you set aside committed time together. Accomplishing your SMART goals will not happen passively. You will need to make an effort outside of day-to-day tasks. The cadence of the meeting schedule will vary based on your goals and timeline. A behavioral change may take longer to achieve. You may have multiple SMART goals to reach your endpoint, with each SMART goal building on the prior goal. A desired outcome may be overwhelming unless it is broken down into smaller steps.

The duration of the relationship is variable. A SMART goal like the example above can conclude the mentor-mentee relationship after presentation to the executive team on June 4th. The relationship may continue with new goals. The Executive team has approved your request for a trial of a hospital-at-home program. You have a new concern, as you have never implemented a new program or built a project plan. Is this the right mentor for the next steps? Maybe your mentor leaves the facility. Can you continue the relationship without revealing confidential health system information? Each situation is unique, requiring reassessments over time.

When the formal relationship closes, place a debrief on the agenda. Both you and your mentor will be enlightened, looking back at what went well, areas of opportunity for improvement, and best of all, your growth through the process. The quality of the mentor's guidance will be influenced by your open feedback for future relationships. This segment is as important as goal setting, choosing the right mentor, and having regular meetings.

A word of caution: have an awareness of balancing your work, your job, personal obligations, and the mentorship. Most physicians reading this book are hard-wired to be driven individuals. You may attempt to solve too many issues at once, engaging with multiple mentors. In addition to burnout, this behavior can be viewed as a lack of focus. The perception of being unfocused usually does not lead to leadership or career advancement.

There will be a special bond between you and your mentor. Communication with my mentors continued beyond the formal mentorship. Requesting a mentor is a sign of strength and not weakness. Have the strength and the courage to be mentored.

In addition to numerous books and articles, if you want to dive deeper, The Science of Effective Mentorship in STEMM, published by the National Academies Press, expands on mentorship relationships: (https://www.ncbi.nlm.nih.gov/books/NBK552775/#:~:text=Mentorship%20is%20a%20professional%2C%20working,of%20career%20and%20psychosocial%20support).

THE SPARK BEHIND MY CURIOSITY

Bahar Sedarati, MD, CPE, FCUCM

https://www.linkedin.com/in/baharsedaratimd/

The following words eloquently express the importance of great role models and mentors. Bahar Sedarati has dedicated many years of study to this critical topic. I am indebted to her for sharing her learnings here.

I love learning. Always have. But it wasn't born from abundance — it came from absence. Growing up without strong mentors or role models left a noticeable gap. One I couldn't quite name at the time, but I felt it. That gap sparked a relentless curiosity — an urge to grow, to understand, to find better ways of being — and eventually, to pass that growth along to others.

Later in life, discovering what it truly means to have a mentor changed everything. For the first time, I felt genuinely seen and invested in. I was cared for, not for what I would perform, but for who I could become. That feeling of being believed in? It satisfied a deep, quiet thirst I didn't even know I was carrying.

Maybe that's why I've become such an avid reader. This past year, I found myself deeply immersed in the work of Carol Dweck and David Yeager. Their ideas gave language to something I had intuitively felt but never fully articulated. They helped me shift from performing to becoming, from perfectionism to potential.

From Performance to Potential

We live in a world obsessed with performance. It's easy to slip into the trap of treating people like projects — measuring worth by output. I've done it. I've been on both ends of it.

That's why the research of Dweck and Yeager struck such a chord. They reminded me: people aren't products to be optimized. They're potential in progress. And the way we speak to others — especially when they're struggling — can either unlock that potential or shut it down.

Three ideas from their work now shape how I lead, teach, and show up: **Wise Feedback,** the **Mentor Mindset,** and the **Growth Mindset.**

Wise Feedback: Challenge with Care

Imagine receiving tough feedback that doesn't sting — but inspires. That's wise feedback.

David Yeager's research shows that when feedback includes both high expectations and a deep belief in someone's potential, it becomes transformational. He defines **Wise Feedback** as:

High Standards + High Support + Clear Belief in Belonging and Potentials

It sounds like this:

"I'm giving you this feedback because I know you're capable of reaching a higher standard, and I believe in your ability to get there. I'm here to help you succeed."

This framing doesn't threaten a person's identity. Instead, it frames feedback as a vote of confidence. Not a judgment — but an investment.

The Mentor Mindset: Holding the Tension

David Yeager also offers a simple, profound 2x2 framework that helped me rethink how I mentor and lead:

Y-axis: Support — Do I believe in your potential, and will I support your growth?

X-axis: Standards — Do I believe you can and should reach a meaningful goal?

This framework yields four types of responses:

Neglectful (Low Standards, Low Support): "It doesn't matter, and you probably can't do it anyway."

Enforcer (High Standards, Low Support): "You must meet the bar — but you're on your own."

Protector (Low Standards, High Support): "I care, so I'll lower the bar to protect you from pressure."

Mentor (High Standards, High Support): "This matters — and I believe you can do it. I'll help you rise."

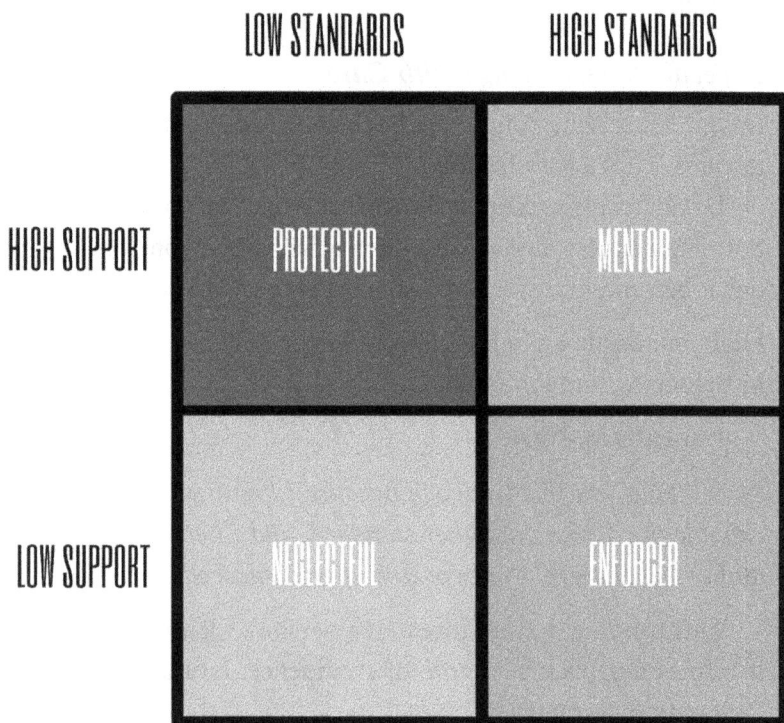

	LOW STANDARDS	HIGH STANDARDS
HIGH SUPPORT	PROTECTOR	MENTOR
LOW SUPPORT	NEGLECTFUL	ENFORCER

The **Mentor Mindset** holds the tension between care and challenge. It says:

"I won't lower the bar. But I'll walk beside you as you climb."

I've worked with mentors like that — people who saw in me what I couldn't yet see in myself. And I've also experienced the opposite — leaders who withheld belief or support, sometimes unknowingly.

Now, I choose to lead differently.

The Growth Mindset: Fuel for Becoming

At the heart of both wise feedback and the mentor mindset is Carol Dweck's idea of a **Growth Mindset** — the belief that skills and intelligence aren't fixed traits, but can grow with effort, strategy, and support.

People with a growth mindset:

- View mistakes as learning opportunities.
- Embrace challenges instead of avoiding them.
- Use feedback as fuel, not a personal attack.
- Believe their brain can change, because neuroscience shows it can.

This mindset changes everything. It reshapes how we learn, how we teach, and how we bounce back from failure.

Final Thought: Lead Like a Mentor

When we lead with wise feedback, adopt the mentor mindset, and model a growth mindset, we stop seeing people as they are and start seeing them for who they can become.

That's what real leadership is.

Not fixing. Not rescuing.
But believing. Challenging. Walking alongside.

Because the most transformational leaders — and the most remarkable humans — build bridges between belief and potential. That's where growth lives. That's where people bloom.

And maybe that's why I've always been curious: because deep down, I believed there was more. I just needed someone to believe it with me.

Coaches

Much of what was covered for mentors applies to coaches with a few key differences. Executive or professional coaches are paid to provide objective mentorship. They have special training allowing them to serve as professional coaches. You may hire a coach, or your employer may provide you with a coach. When an employer provides the coach, it is often because the employer wants to elevate you to be the best you. They see something in you that they believe brings value to the company. An employer would not invest in your growth otherwise. If you are asked to perform a leadership role or task and do not feel prepared, you can request a coach from your employer.

I have seen coaches hired to work with executive teams. They may observe meetings and then provide feedback to the group or individuals. The role of the coach in this circumstance is to enhance the outcomes of the team.

Executive coaches may be unfamiliar with your industry or the specifics of your day-to-day job. This fact is not important to cultivate a great partnership with you. They are focused on your future goals, identifying the roadblocks standing in your way. They help you identify triggers that motivate your behaviors. Their strategy is to unblock obstacles, helping guide you in a forward direction, bridging the gap between where you are today and where you want to be tomorrow.

We are all shaped, to some extent, by past experiences. If a past experience needs resolution before you can move forward, as it may still be a source of mental anguish and cause a roadblock, you may need to seek care from a behavioral health therapist in addition to your coach. Executive coaches focus their efforts on helping you achieve a goal moving forward.

Coaches typically do not give you all the answers. A great coach helps you recognize or bring awareness to a behavior that you are not mindful of. They take the situation and help you work through the present state of affairs. Do you recall the saying, "If you do not think of the diagnosis, you will not make the diagnosis?" In simple terms, if a patient has a given illness and you do not include it in your differential diagnosis, you will not make the correct diagnosis. Coaches will observe behaviors that you may not recognize in yourself. In essence, they will make a "diagnosis" you did not consider.

You will find a greater selection of executive or professional coaches from which to choose in contrast to the supply of mentors. Beware, however: Many individuals will tout themselves as being leadership coaches. Check their credentials. Seek out a coach who is certified by the International Coaching Federation (ICF). This certification is obtained by rigorous training and includes an oath to uphold a code of ethics, ethical standards, and core values of the ICF. The ICF has a database of coaches, which is one of many resources to help you identify a potential coach. Checking the credentials of anyone advertising professional coaching increases your likelihood of choosing a qualified executive coach.

Interview several coaches before making a final selection. Identify how each coach operates and if your goals align with their techniques. Does the relationship feel suitable enough to commence a partnership? It may not be love at first sight, but at least you'll know if a second date is on the horizon or if you prefer to break up after the initial meeting. Coaches are interviewing you at the same time. A good coach will only accept clients if the fit is good. A professional coach will not feel rejected if you do your homework and opt for a different coach at the end of the selection process.

Coaching does come with a financial price tag. However, an investment in yourself is a wise investment. If you cannot afford a personal coach, consider group coaching. Stay tuned, as AI coaching is on the horizon.

I'll end this chapter with one of my proudest mentorship moments with respect to career growth and advancement. I was the interim medical director for a recently launched market. The launch was anything but smooth due to unanticipated factors. The market included one nurse practitioner whose reaction to feedback was harsh attacks and threats. I cannot pinpoint what I saw in this person, but fortunately I saw something. Over the months and years that followed, this person went from a market clinician with a strong voice among her peers to a leader in the company. I later learned she started her medical career homeless. I have never been so proud of an individual's resolve to better herself through mentorship.

IN SUMMARY:

1. There are different levels of support to help you on your quest to reach your goals. These include preceptors, mentors, and coaches. The available options progress in enhancing your outcomes as you press forward.

2. Reflect on what makes a great preceptor or mentor. Emulate those behaviors when precepting or coaching others. Look for those characteristics when selecting a mentor or coach.

3. Ensure a mentor has the experience you seek to be effective in developing your skill sets.

4. Be clear on your outcomes and goals from a mentor or coach experience. SMART goals are a gold standard for achieving the best results.

5. Define the "rules of engagement" at the start of a mentorship relationship, allowing for a safe space and a trusting relationship.

6. You must put the effort into a preceptor, mentor, or coaching relationship for a positive end-product.
7. Efficacious relationships are open, honest, objective, and non-defensive.
8. When choosing a professional or executive coach, ensure they are certified by the International Coaching Federation.
9. Interview multiple coaches to select the optimal person to benefit your personal goals.
10. Investing in the services of a professional coach is a wise investment for your personal growth.

Is MD or DO Enough?

LETTERS

D id you ever look at someone's signature line on an email, title on a business card, or LinkedIn profile and notice they have alphabet soup after their name? The font size may be different than the rest of the business card to fit everything on the card. I am likely dating myself, as QR codes and digital business cards are replacing traditional business cards, but you get the point.

John Doe, MD, PhD, MBA, CPE, FACS, FACC, MACP, FACR,
*   Pharm D*
President, Greatest Medical Association
Immediate Past CEO, Cure Cancer Today
Past CMO, Health Excellence Primary Care
Acupuncture and Massage Therapy Certified

Do you know the designation of each set of letters after John Doe's name in the above example? Many physicians can likely figure it out, while a layperson looks at it in awe. This physician earned a doctorate of medicine (can be a DO as opposed to MD, meaning a doctorate in osteopathy), a doctorate of philosophy (has likely done medical research), a master's in business administration, is a certified physician executive, designated a fellow member in the American College of Surgeons, a fellow member in the American College of Cardiology, a master member in the American College of Physicians, a fellow member in the American College of Radiology, and has a doctorate in pharmacology.

This is one accomplished person! Look at all the letters after their name and at all the high-level executive positions they've held. You cannot wait to be this person one day.

Let's take a deeper dive. How did this individual find the time to earn all these degrees and hold all the listed jobs? Why did they complete so many residencies in different fields? As the hiring manager, I would want to know the answer to these questions. It makes sense to be double-boarded in some areas, such as a surgeon who specializes in breast cancer receiving fellowship training in plastic surgery.

Many physicians are double-boarded in internal medicine and pediatrics, completing med-peds residencies instead of taking the family medicine route, which includes additional areas of training. Either Dr. Doe has great reasons for completing multiple unrelated residencies or he is indecisive and non-committal. He may get bored easily. He may be someone who never feels fulfilled. He may have a thirst for knowledge. I may have concerns as a hiring manager that this individual will not become engaged enough to stay with my company for any significant amount of time. Will this person be able to focus on the tasks at hand? Will this person be disruptive to the company's culture?

Next is their involvement in association work. Fellowship designations are medical professional associations' method of recognition of excellence and dedication to the profession. In many associations that bestow fellowships, you must remain a member of the association to use the fellowship designation; therefore, obtaining fellowship contributes to the financial stability of the association via membership dues.

The master's designation in business administration (MBA) and master's in the American College of Physicians (MACP) are difficult to attain and earn the holder a higher degree of respect.

Is having an MBA valuable to your career success? Maybe. An MBA is a significant investment of your time and money. Depending on where you are in your career, you may need to cut back on your income-generating work hours to obtain your MBA. Conversely, you may receive a promotion or salary increase at your current job after completing an MBA. You will never go wrong obtaining an MBA or any ongoing education for that matter. Expanding your knowledge base, applying it to your career or outside of your career, is triumphant, no matter how you slice it.

An MBA is not your only option. If you Google "physician leadership programs," you will get lists of options, including but not limited to, MBA programs, certified physician executive (CPE), one-off courses in physician leadership, LEAD programs, leadership development by medical specialties, high-level C-suite physician development programs, and many others. I encourage you to explore the multitude of options, weighing the upsides and downsides of each. You will find some degree of benefit from any additional leadership training. We explore this more fully in the section below.

This physician has been a CMO and a CEO! That is certainly impressive. You research the companies where this person held these roles and learn the CMO role was at a private practice of two physicians, three nurse practitioners, and one physician assistant. You learn that Cure Cancer Today is a nonprofit fundraising group established by two men whose wives were recently diagnosed with breast cancer. Dr. Doe served as CEO for a time, lending his expertise as a physician.

Your research could have turned up completely different scenarios, causing you to view Dr. Doe in a different light. What if he started in the CMO position as the founder of Health Excellence Primary Care, which grew to more than 3,000 employees and covered two million lives? The company went public, and the stock continues to increase in value. Dr. Doe's success as CMO led to his CEO position at Cure Cancer Today, where he took a company functioning at a loss and turned it around into a profitable company that was later purchased by a well-respected larger company.

These are two very different scenarios illustrating that letters after a name may or may not be helpful in your job search.

MBA vs. CPE vs. FACHE

Master of Business Administration (MBA)

MBA programs come in many flavors and varieties, and one size does not fit all. There are traditional MBA programs to which anyone can apply. These may be full-time traditional programs, which are usually two years in length. Some alternative programs are part-time or online, self-paced, and may take 3-5 years for completion.

The physician executive MBA programs are designed to better meet physician needs. For example, some programs allow you to work at your own pace. Some programs are fully remote with instructor-led sessions in addition to self-learning. They may establish cohorts for projects and other support throughout the program. The program can be an accelerated structured one-year program or a slower-paced 2–3-year program. You may or may not be required to participate in some onsite educational activities. Professors often understand the nature of your "day" job and are more willing to accommodate reasonable assignment due dates.

The differences between a traditional MBA program and a physician executive MBA program may be more than how the program is delivered. Both programs include the same core areas of study, such as finance, supply chain, and business plan development, for example. The physician executive MBA uses examples or case studies relevant to medicine. For example, the physician MBA program may study how health systems expanded their programs internationally or how they turned a poor-performing practice/hospital into a high performer in finances as well as culture. Your assignments may allow you to apply real-life situations you are facing, where you and expert professors help develop solutions. You are bolstering your resume during your MBA studies by developing and implementing successful projects.

There are additional advantages to an interactive physician MBA program versus the self-directed learning programs. You are with a group of like-minded individuals who become your MBA family. You lift each other up and form a bond. Instead of trudging through assignments alone, usually at odd hours, you have communication with others frequently working these same hours. You help each other, catering to the strengths and weaknesses of those in your cohort group, ensuring each person attains the necessary skills for success. This new MBA family stays with you for life. I am 10 years out from earning my MBA and am still in contact with many of my classmates as we help each other through difficult work situations, celebrate each other's personal and professional successes, or network.

Choose an MBA program that is right for you. One size does not fit all. I chose a one-year accelerated program. I was a medical director at two facilities: one in an emergency department and one in an urgent care center. I resigned from the urgent care medical director role to relieve the time restraints required for a one-year program.

I had the full support of my family as they understood the financial impacts and the secluded, non-social life I would live for that year. I did not believe I could push through two years; a faster-paced one-year program was more enticing to me. I needed a structured program to ensure I had the discipline to complete it.

Certified Physician Executive (CPE)

The American Association for Physician Leadership (AAPL) offers the Certified Physician Executive (CPE). More than 4,000 physicians have earned a CPE as of January 2025. It is not an MBA, yet it offers many similar components. Some advantages of a CPE include the following: There are 125 hours of core components in the program. Required optional classes fill out the remainder of the requirements. In other words, you choose 30 hours of elective courses, from 60 hours of options, that benefit you the most, be it areas of weakness or areas that best match your present or future goals. This is a self-paced program. The cost is significantly less than an MBA program. You can attend some live AAPL sessions for CPE credit or complete the online or virtual sessions.

The program culminates with a capstone project. To qualify for the CPE capstone, you must complete the required coursework, be a licensed physician with active or past recognized board certification, be an active member of AAPL for at least a year (which you will attain as you complete the coursework leading up to the capstone), and be a practicing clinician for at least three years beyond residency and fellowship training. You can start the coursework prior to qualifying for the capstone, but the qualifications must be met by the time you apply for the capstone.

This CPE capstone is different from an MBA capstone. The MBA capstone requires you to complete a focused project under the guidance of an adviser. The CPE capstone consists of five assignments that are sent to the cohort leader for feedback and modification requests. These assignments are combined into a professional five-minute presentation in front of a panel of professionals. A passing score on the presentation is required to graduate. This five-minute presentation is harder than it sounds, as you must be concise, communicating a lot of information in a short time span.

Your CPE cohort is formed during the capstone timeframe and does not come together as a group at the start of the program. AAPL allows for capstones to be completed at one of four dates annually, virtually or in person. You will be recognized for your achievement, walking on stage at the awards ceremony held during the annual convention, and with the CPE designation on your signature line.

There are some modifications for physicians who already hold an MBA degree. The qualifications do change periodically, so check the website (https://www.physicianleaders.org/credentials/cpe) as you explore your options.

Table 1 provides a general summary of the differences between the three options, (MBA, physician executive MBA, and CPE). Offerings and requirements are always changing. Do your research. Determine what fits your needs and learning style the best.

TABLE 1. Comparison of Traditional MBA, Physician Executive MBA, and CPE

	Traditional MBA	Physician Executive MBA	Certified Physician Executive (CPE)
Core master's level required business courses	yes	yes	
Core plus optional choice required business courses			yes
Physician or healthcare focused		yes	yes
Admission requirements	yes	yes	yes
Cost	$$$	$$	$
Duration	variable	variable	variable
In-person only	an option	an option	
Virtual only	an option	an option	an option
Self-paced	an option	an option	an option
Hybrid in-person and virtual	an option	an option	an option
Graduation recognition	diploma, walk, hooding ceremony	diploma, walk, hooding ceremony	certificate, walk, recognition ceremony

Do you need an MBA or CPE? Again, the answer is "maybe." You can apply the knowledge you gain by obtaining the MBA or CPE at your job or at home. On-the-job experience is not equal to a degree or certification — but the two go hand in hand. Having the degree and letters after your name brings little value if you have difficulty applying the newly learned skills. We engage in continuous learning because times change, advancements are made, and the expertise needed almost always leaves room for continued personal development. Pairing an MBA or CPE with experience brings exponential value.

After I obtained my MBA, I was told that I presented differently, my thought process was different. I realized that I now had the understanding to identify the necessary components of providing excellent clinical care and how to present these needs in a way that made business sense. I learned a new language that allowed me to effectively communicate with both the clinicians and operators/executive teams. Speaking the language of the C-suite garners greater respect. I can look at both the clinical and operational sides of a business objectively. I analyze downstream impacts.

What is the value of also being a CPE? This question is frequently posted on the AAPL discussion board, and the responses are nearly unanimous: The MBA and CPE complement each other. Many physicians who obtained an MBA and then the CPE remark that they wish they had obtained their CPE sooner. They recognize that the CPE is more physician-focused, more focused on people management, and helps optimize effective leadership styles.

I participated in a physician executive MBA program that provided some of the additional benefits of the CPE curriculum; however, the CPE is more comprehensive. Effective people management is not recognized as a critical, time-consuming, high-priority task until you are sitting in the seat of an administrative position. Many physicians determine that the CPE meets their needs and do not pursue an MBA.

Fellow of the American College of Healthcare Executives (FACHE)

Another continuing education option to consider is the Fellowship of the American College of Healthcare Executives (FACHE). This certification focuses on healthcare management and is not just for physicians. Fellows must pass an exam to become "board certified" in healthcare management. To qualify for the exam, you must first be a member of the American College of Healthcare Executives (ACHE). Additional qualifications include holding an advanced degree (MD and DO qualify). You must currently hold an executive healthcare management position and have a minimum of five years of healthcare management experience. You will need to submit two references. You are required to complete 36 hours of continuing education credits, of which 12 must be in person from the ACHE. Finally, you need to have been involved in four volunteer activities, two of which are in community or civic service and two that are healthcare-related.

Candidates have three years to meet the requirements prior to taking the Board of Governors Exam in Healthcare Management. The cost to apply in 2025 is $250 with an exam fee of $225. Additional costs include membership in the association, registration fee for the in-person conferences, and fees for the additional educational credit courses. ACHE provides many sources and services at additional fees to prepare for the exam.

The exam is 230 questions, with 200 questions scored and 30 presented as trial questions for potential future exams. Up to six hours is allotted for exam completion. Testing is completed at a secure testing site and results are immediately shared with the candidate. The exam must be passed within two years of submitting the application. Candidates may take the exam as many times as needed to pass, paying an additional exam fee for each attempt and allowing a 60-day wait period between exam attempts.

Unlike an MBA or CPE, members who hold the **FACHE designation must recertify every three years** by completing continuing education or by retaking the Board of Governors exam with a $350 fee for each attempt. There is a $200 recertification application fee separate from the exam fee. The same community service requirement is in place for the time period from your initial FACHE certification or last recertification to the time of the present recertification. ACHE does have some fee waivers for qualifying individuals and other nuances. Like obtaining the CPE or other certifications, check the website for updates in requirements, which are reviewed by the organizations routinely: https://www.ache.org/fache.

Additional Considerations

There are myriad other degrees and certifications you might consider. One size does not fit all. If you choose a path in epidemiology, a Master of Public Health (MPH) may be your best option. Many medical specialty associations have leadership tracks with a variety of certifications possible. I find these options often serve as an introduction to a leadership trajectory. They bring great value for an early-career physician leader. Even as a seasoned physician leader, I usually have some takeaways when I participate in these sessions. Leadership development never ends. I recommend attending as many leadership trainings as possible.

Identify your passion, which is often aligned with your SMART goal(s). Seek out additional niche training to support your goal. It may be risk management, compliance, or coding to informatics, artificial intelligence, or a huge range of possibilities in between. Many physicians are familiar with the legal bucket. Many of us know physicians who are also lawyers. Are you aware there's a Master of Legal Studies (MLS) in health? These programs are designed for non-lawyer health professionals with an emphasis on health law, policy, and management. If you want to take it a step further, consider an Executive Juris Doctor (EJD) degree. Like those with an MLS degree, these professionals do not intend to practice law and do not sit for the bar exam.

What about opportunities such as board positions or volunteer roles within the healthcare system or company that enhance your resume but do not add letters to your name? I repeat: All experiences are good experiences, as they add to your capabilities. The first consideration is how much time you have to give versus the return on time investment.

There are many different levels of board positions. Most healthcare systems have a medical board. These positions can be elected by the medical staff or, at smaller hospitals, frequently appointed, with the chairs of each department staffing the board. Start-up companies may have board positions open to investors or in exchange for equity.

Consider getting involved with your specialty association. I speak from the heart on this topic as I have been involved with the American College of Physicians since the start of my residency in 1990. These associations support you with education, advocacy, resources, and many unmeasured secondary gains. Some of my best mentors, such as Dr. Ammazzalorso, sprouted from association connections. When you become involved, your opportunities for networking expand. You may start by chairing a committee or performing other volunteer work for the association before you run for a board position. You can choose your areas of interest. For example, if you are interested in politics, advocacy may be your path, allowing you to network with governmental policymakers. These positions are almost always volunteer situations. Travel and meeting expenses are usually covered once you attain a board position.

Most boards or association positions provide, at a minimum, an introduction to business concepts. You need to understand budgeting and finances in these roles. Strategic planning should be a component of association management. It is hard to place a price on these downstream impacts, as I cannot recall a time when I did not benefit.

Volunteering in your healthcare system or company has less clarity. If the opportunity aligns with your values and brings you joy, it's a no-brainer. For example, let's say you have a child who suffered from leukemia. Developing a fundraising event with profits supporting the Leukemia Society or participating in a foundation fundraising event benefiting the hospital's cancer center, all make sense. There are many volunteer committees in your healthcare system. Once your value on these committees is realized, you will be asked to join more and more committees, including serving as a chair. You will find it hard to say no when asked, as you do not want to let anyone down. My recommendation is to strategically accept opportunities that will provide growth or mentorship that align with your SMART goals. I recommend reading *The Power of a Positive No: How to Say No and Still Get to Yes* by William Ury.

IN SUMMARY:

1. Additional degrees and/or certifications will complement your medical degree, while experience combined with these degrees brings exponential value.
2. You cannot go wrong by expanding your business comprehension and leadership skill sets.
3. The options to acquire these additional areas of expertise are numerous.
    a. Match your needs to progress down your chosen career path, advancement, or change with the benefits each program provides.
    b. Do your research on different programs.
    c. Include financial and work-life balance in your decision-making.
4. A degree or certification alone does not equal competency in the subject matter that the degree or certification represents.
5. Consider board and volunteer positions if they support your SMART goals.

It's a Big World Out There

FOCUS

Let's say you've decided you want to make a change from your current day-to-day role. What does that change look like? Do you want to move up the career hierarchy> Maybe you're a medical director and want to move toward becoming a chief medical officer (CMO). Or maybe you're burned out with 80-hour workweeks in patient care and are looking to get "out" of medicine. Does that mean you want to move out of the medical field entirely and start a new career in a different industry? Do you want to move away from direct patient care and into the pharma, research, payer, or industry realms? Perhaps you want to attend law school and use your medical knowledge in the legal world. The choices are endless, from where you practice to accountabilities to how you spend your time each day.

As you contemplate the direction you want to take, there are many factors to consider. Some of the more significant concepts to contemplate are discussed in this chapter. Writing your goals down as SMART goals will help guide you. It's helpful to think about where you want to be one, three, five, and 10 years from now, then develop short-term stepping-stone goals between today and a more complex long-term ultimate goal. What you set out to accomplish may diverge from the grand plan because your priorities or values change, or innovation creates advancements with new opportunities. What's the pot of gold at the end of the rainbow that will bring you happiness?

Define Success

It's important to reflect on the difference between success and happiness. A person may view success through the lens of material objects or appearances: "Jane is successful because she has a high-paying job, a great house, an awesome car, and she takes amazing vacations." That might all be true, but if you ask Jane whether she's

79

successful with all of those checkmarks, she may say no. Jane may tell you she rarely eats dinner with her family, she misses important family events, and she feels like she must be her best at all times because others are always looking at her and judging her. She feels stressed and alone.

Now let's consider Joe. Joe has a full-time job, lives in a modest home, has a nice car, and can meet all the basic needs for himself and his family. He takes a family vacation annually and can invest money toward retirement. Joe is able to attend important events in his children's lives and is often at the dinner table. Between Joe and Jane, Joe is likely happier even though he doesn't have the same assets as Jane. Each person must determine their own definition of success. My definition has significantly changed over the years based on my personal experiences. I now define success as happiness.

That brings us to the first decision point: What does success look like for you? There are no right or wrong answers. If success means owning material items, that's great, as it's *your* definition of success. A person who loves the outdoors may not view a penthouse apartment in a large city as a reward for their success, but *you* may view it that way. Don't judge your own beliefs so long as they don't harm others. In the chapter "What's Stopping You?" we discussed values and the notion that many people who enter the medical profession do so based on a calling to help others. If you value material items and financial worth, that does not mean you also have a calling to help others. You can provide exceptional patient care and experiences while creating financial wealth for yourself.

In that same vein, look at what brings you happiness and how that relates to your career choices. Are you someone who likes to build teams or programs, or would you rather maintain them? Do you like ambiguity, or do you thrive with structure? Do you enjoy working from home or do you need in-person interactions with others? Are you a team person or an individual contributor? Does a long commute bring you happiness if you can live somewhere you desire, like a lake house, and allow yourself time to decompress following a stress-filled day? Or do you get annoyed by long commutes?

It took me a long time to learn and admit to myself that I get bored easily, so I need a job with more ambiguity, where I can build and not just sustain, and where there's a lot of change. Hence, I enjoy startup or growth companies over academic institutions. In retrospect, that's most likely why I practiced emergency medicine for over 20 years despite being trained in internal medicine. I planned to stay in the emergency department for one year, but that was clearly not what happened!

Values

Values form the foundation for most choices. Having a clear hold on your own personal values is essential, as discussed in the chapter "What's Stopping You?" Sometimes you must compromise on your decisions, but you should not compromise on your values. For example, you may value engaging in a healthy daily lifestyle routine, but you've traveled across the country for an offsite meeting and your obligations prohibit you from getting the amount of sleep you value for that healthy lifestyle. Maybe you must forego exercising for a day because the hotel gym doesn't open early enough. The day is packed with meetings and activities from early morning to late evening. You haven't changed your value of wanting to live a healthy daily routine, but you did need to make concessions for a day. And while one "off" day might be okay, daily deviations wouldn't be sustainable. Make a list of your top three to five values and ensure that your career choice supports these values.

Strengths and Weaknesses

You need to understand your strengths and weaknesses. I love music, but I know I'll never be a true rock star musician because I lack the gene for musical talent. Evaluating your strengths and weaknesses will help you align with the right-fitting role. And remember that your strength is often your greatest weakness, as we already discussed. For example, one of my strengths is my energy, but it can be exhausting for others. Your strength may not be something you enjoy doing, and that can place pressure on you because other people will insist that you can't let that talent go to waste. Think of an exceptional athlete: Whether they want to or not, they're pushed and pushed to continue in their sport. High expectations are placed on them. It's hard for such an athlete to state that they don't enjoy their sport, especially if it has been part of their fabric since childhood.

Experience

On the flip side, you can develop a weakness into a strength, or at a minimum, you can gain some knowledge in that area. As you evaluate where you want to be in five or 10 years, look at the skills you need to demonstrate as you pave a path toward your career goals. If leadership roles are in your future, consider taking physician leadership courses from the American Association for Physician Leadership (AAPL) or doing other similar training. Each endpoint will require a different set of skills, so determine what the stepping stones are from point A to point B and get started on your journey.

If after you set out, you find you chose the wrong path, recognize that you have gained experience and knowledge on the journey, and it is not too late to plot a new course. Examine objectively why the first path did not guide you in the best direction, so you avoid going around in circles. Bumps in the road are expected. Embrace each of these bumps as added opportunities for growth.

What if you already have the training and you need the experience? Seek out opportunities. Contact mentors or others in your organization or community. Share your needs and inquire about projects you could take on or other opportunities for you to gain experience. This is often an unbudgeted request and you likely won't receive monetary compensation. However, the compensation is in the form of opportunity and experience, which you can add to your résumé when you apply for a job that requires that specific expertise.

Transitioning from Clinical to Non-Clinical

The decision to transition from a clinical role to a non-clinical position can be difficult. Even in the case where the choice is obvious, it is likely you will wade through a sea of emotions. Imagine yourself as a surgeon. You suffer a stroke that limits the mobility of your dominant hand. You can no longer continue as a surgeon who "cuts" on people; however, you might consider clinical patient care that does not require performing procedures, although examining a patient may be difficult without use of your dominant hand. You can dictate notes, so that will not be a problem. You cannot supervise residents in the operating room, as you cannot step into the case if necessary

You might consider running the resident clinic, but that position has never excited you. For years, you fantasized about building a tool to expedite a certain procedure in the OR. You have an idea of what that tool should look like and the function it should perform. You approach a medical device company that is excited to explore designing and developing this device with you. You still identify yourself as a surgeon yet hesitate in identifying yourself as a surgeon to others.

I can share story after story of my MBA classmates struggling with leaving the clinical arena for an administrative job. If I don't use my clinical skills, will I lose this skill set? Do I lose my identification as a specific type of physician? Do I continue to maintain my board certification? What if I am not successful in a non-clinical role? Will I enjoy being an administrator? Although I cannot answer these questions for you, I will share my thoughts.

First, your experience in the clinical world can never be stripped from you. That is a part of your fabric, although your skill sets may dull over time. I was an emergency department physician for over 20 years. Despite not practicing emergency medicine for more than 10 years, I am still a physician with 20-plus years of emergency medicine experience. No one can take that away from me.

My biggest fear was giving up a well-paying job that I enjoyed but that did not excite me anymore, for a non-clinical, lower-paying job. I knew the path I would take, opting to explore non-clinical or less-clinical options. My choice came down to two possibilities: CEO for a large urgent care company wishing to expand nationally or medical director for implementation with Landmark Health, a start-up private equity-based company. I was enthusiastic as the CEO interviews progressed, recognizing that although I had never been a CEO, I did have the skill sets to excel in the role. Yet, I was apprehensive, fearing I would fail. A friend, who is also a professional executive coach, helped me recognize that I could not fail by taking on the new role of CEO. Even if it was not a good fit and I left the new position, I would still gain irreplaceable experience for my future career. The start-up company could go belly-up or experience financial hardships, requiring the elimination of my position.

Ultimately, before the CEO offer was even made, I chose to join Landmark Health based on what would bring me the greatest fulfillment. Landmark aligned with my values perfectly. I never looked back with regrets or "what if." Consider your personality. I could feel burnout creeping in, working full-time, 12-hour shifts in the emergency department, in addition to serving as the medical director. I was relieved when I could step away from patient care and focus on being medical director, but just a few hours sitting behind a desk had me clamoring to get up out of the chair and care for patients. What benefits do you get from patient contact? Can you be happy without those benefits? Can you fill the void elsewhere? Is there an option for a hybrid role while you test out a distinctly different choice?

Keeping your hand in patient care to some degree has benefits if there is an option to do so. If clinical physicians report to you, you will gain their respect by continuing some patient care responsibilities. For example, you may not take call as frequently, but stepping into the call schedule will earn their praise. You will experience much of what your reports experience. It will be easier to identify and relate to their concerns. Negotiations, when problem-solving, become less cumbersome. In addition, doing some clinical hours, especially early in your transition from clinical to non-clinical, may allow you to better negotiate an acceptable salary. I personally believe physicians in administrative roles generate a greater ROI.

I initially retained a few clinical hours after joining Landmark Health, for both business needs and personal satisfaction. I related better to my team's individual challenges and the rewards they felt caring for patients in their homes. I presented better at business development meetings with clients, relying on my experience in the field.

I was able to step in and perform patient care during unforeseen circumstances, limiting disruption to the care our patients received.

My very conscientious direct reports were grateful when I stepped in for them at times of need. In exchange, they were loyal and beyond cooperative with my asks of them far beyond my expectation. New workflows developed from these experiences that improved efficiencies and quality of care.

A friend was an excellent elementary school teacher in an underserved district where male teachers were scarce for this age group. He was asked to consider an administrative role in the district. It weighed heavily on him as he recognized that these young male children with limited positive role models needed him in their lives. A superintendent in another district suggested that he would have a much greater impact on these students in the administrative role. Instead of having a positive impact on 30 students annually, he would mentor many other teachers and develop programs with constructive outcomes, spreading a wider net of influence on these young students.

There is significant controversy surrounding renewal of board certification, which will not be addressed here. Suffice it to say that I believe the benefits of maintaining board certification outweigh the risks. Employment in non-academic settings may take you further away from the latest updates in medicine unless you make a concerted effort to stay abreast of these changes. Complex schedules can impede the best intentions. You may be in a position where you supervise advanced practice providers or where you need to be credentialed with payers yourself, even if you have a very small patient panel. Retaining board certification simplifies these situations. If you allow your board certification to lapse, you must overcome many hurdles to achieve it again. I find board certification crucial for my career.

Let's examine another subject with respect to the transition from clinical to administrative responsibilities. You have worked as a clinician for years. When you transition to an administrative role in the same system or company, your former peers may now view you as "one of them." How do you balance maintaining friendships, being respected, and having a positive impact, all while implementing strategic plans for the company?

First, recognize that your key stakeholders have changed. Previously, your key stakeholders were your patients, their families or caregivers, the patient care team, and your supervisor. In your new administrative position, you maintain all the prior key stakeholders and add the C-suite, a board of directors, and possibly, investors. How can you possibly please everyone?

Humility will support this transition as you learn and develop new skill sets. Your peers must respect your new role. You need to understand your direct reports' perceptions of higher-level decision-making. There are some facts you will not have the freedom to share with your team in your administrative position. You should reveal as many specifics and data as allowed to impart a better understanding of the decision-making process. Listen, listen, listen to concerns and options to mitigate conflict while navigating to solutions.

Whenever possible, bring a representative group to the solutioning table. One large healthcare system, like so many others, felt the impacts of financial constraints. Unionized nurses demanded a pay raise, surgeons wanted new robotic devices, hospitalists wanted additional nurse practitioners or physician assistants to take overnight call, and so on. The CEO united a group of individuals representing diverse needs. They were given the financial numbers and tasked with developing recommendations. This group emerged with cooperative decision-making to best support patient care, given the financial restraints. Over the next few years, finances improved, and wishes were granted, ultimately having a positive impact on patients and the community. As importantly, a relationship of trust developed between the C-suite and employees.

You need to draw a line between work accountabilities and friendships. In my distant past, the director of the department continued to play poker and go on fishing trips with the male physicians. There was *perceived* favoritism toward the male physicians over the females. He respectfully removed himself from these extracurricular activities when we shared our trepidations with him. He shared with me his perception that being a medical director is a lonely position.

I do not necessarily agree. My recommendation is to be cautious of optics. If an activity or relationship can be perceived as anything less than objective or inclusive, stay away. If a friend needs to be coached or you need to address a potential concern, do it as objectively as you would with any other employee. You can be perceived as weak and ineffective if you cannot have these difficult conversations with *all* your direct reports. Your friend should respect your new professional relationship.

Consider a veteran nurse in the emergency department. They have experienced many clinical situations. They have observed assorted bedside manners, from the emergency department providers to consultants and others managing patient care in the department. Congratulations! This nurse graduated with a master's degree as a nurse practitioner, passed the board exam, and is now hired in the same department.

This nurse may experience resentment in many forms: Some former peer nurses do not like "taking" orders from this nurse practitioner, while others feel they have better clinical judgment than the newly graduated nurse practitioner. Some physicians expect this person to perform at a high level, given their prior experience in the emergency department, not recognizing that this is a very different set of skills and expectations. The newly knighted nurse practitioner feels the pressure to perform to a high standard. Approaching this situation with humility, both in verbal communication and body language, will earn respect.

All the above situations lend themselves to the benefits of mentorship or an executive coach, as you only have one chance at a first impression. A mentor will provide wisdom, helping you traverse the bumps in your new road. In time, you will acquire increasing competencies to manage these bumps.

Do I Stay or Do I Go?

New situation: You like your current organization but feel bored, wanting more of a challenge. Perhaps you feel a bit burned out. You may be discouraged that others are being tapped on the shoulder to advance while you sit idly in your day-in day-out tasks. You may have a great idea but feel frustrated as you are powerless to institute the change. You really don't want to leave but are considering your options to achieve greater satisfaction. Your best option may be to stay with your present organization while orchestrating change to improve your situation. **YOU** need to orchestrate the change despite feeling powerless. It's not as crazy as it sounds.

Where do you begin? A common mistake is not letting your supervisor or the proper individual know you are interested in opportunities outside of your current daily responsibilities. You may have dropped hints. You may think that you will be tapped on the shoulder for an opportunity because you are an exceptional employee. This assumption is costly. The decision makers are as busy as you. They will not take the time to try to determine the desires of others in the organization. Make your wishes clearly known so you and the person sitting next to you have equal opportunities.

It is imperative that you define what you want before making a move. Imagine asking someone for directions if you do not know where you want to go. That is exactly what you are doing if you approach a conversation for change without knowing the desired outcome.

What is the exception to this rule? You may ask your mentor, who may be your supervisor, to help you shape your thoughts into concrete outcomes. You may recognize you need a change but not be able to place your finger on exactly what that change could look like. Working with your mentor or executive coach, you can wade through your thoughts and eventually land on a specific option or options, landing you in a better place to enact a strategy moving forward.

Once you have solidified your desired outcome, develop your SMART goals — defined in great depth in the chapter "Mentorship and Coaching." You are now ready to share. Your immediate super-visor is most likely the best person to approach. If your immediate supervisor is not the one you will discuss your plan with, at least make them aware of your intent. You do not want to leave your supervisor in the dark, learning about changes in your career from another individual. Do not approach your supervisor in the hall-way or in public. You want dedicated time where you will not be interrupted and have the undivided attention of your supervisor.

Consider launching this discussion during a routine 1:1 or private conversation. Ask if you could place this topic on your next agenda. Or send an email requesting a meeting. Requesting time to meet to explore an idea you have in mind, or your future goals, is enough detail to get this meeting on the calendar.

Entering the meeting with a clearly conceptualized appeal is proof that you have a desire that is worth their time. Clearly stating your suggestions is a jumping off point for further discussion, allowing negotiation so both parties benefit. Keep an open mind. You are not privy to all the details about what's going on within the organization. When you state that you are interested in the directorship of the residency program, knowing the current director is about to resign, you may be unaware that there is a plan to reorganize the leadership of multiple residency programs, opening the door for you to apply to a position yet to be posted that better meets your needs.

Don't threaten to quit if you do not get a desirable outcome. Idle threats are not amicable to a strong working relationship. Quitting, or threatening to quit, displays a lack of engagement as well as immaturity. Many supervisors will decide they are better off without you on the team. At a minimum, they will not want to invest time and energy helping you acquire skills or the outcome you desire if your plan is to leave the organization. And if you do choose to leave the organization, the chance that you will receive a positive reference is doubtful.

There may not be an opportunity at the present time, and searching elsewhere for these opportunities may be your ultimate end-product. Your supervisor should understand this choice, allowing you to depart on great terms. This happened to me when a company for which I was employed was faced with unexpected financial constraints, halting all promotions for a number of years. The leadership team in my division was overwhelmingly supportive of me transitioning out of the company for personal growth, which they could not supply.

IN SUMMARY:

1. Define YOUR definition of success.

2. Ascertain your values, strengths, and weaknesses, aligning your career path for greatest success.

3. Transitioning from a clinical to a non-clinical role or from a clinical to an administrative role can be stressful with its own set of emotions and questions.

4. If an opportunity exists within your company or institution to meet your career goals, make your interest known, as your personal goals are not a top priority for decision makers.

5. SMART goals will keep you on track for your desired career trajectory.

Next Steps

EXECUTION

By now, you've done a lot of soul-searching as you've candidly examined your definition of success, what brings you joy and happiness, and which work environments excite you and which ones are an energy drag. You know your strengths and weaknesses, enabling you to develop a plan that addresses knowledge gaps and that aligns with your goals. Let's keep this train moving in the right direction!

PRE-INTERVIEW

Everyone's situation is different, so you need to identify where you see potential barriers to achieving your particular goals, followed by devising a plan to mitigate those barriers. Often, this blueprint starts with enlisting the support of your "key stakeholders." Mine were my family. I needed them to buy into a lifestyle change while I was obtaining my MBA. I would be less available to contribute at home and everyone needed to spend less money, as I decreased my work hours. They not only understood, but they also made extra efforts to complete my usual tasks at home, enabling me to focus on my assignments. On the monetary front, they canceled unnecessary subscriptions, decreased spending, and the like.

Résumé

Once you've satisfied the gaps in your education and experience, it's time to boost your résumé. This is one area where I strongly suggest *not* cutting corners! **Utilizing a professional résumé writer is more than worth the investment, as it will pay off tenfold when you accept the job offer you've been striving to receive.** The last thing you need after working so hard is to *not* stand out positively from other applicants. You need to differentiate yourself as being unquestionably the best candidate in the pool of choices an employer has in front of them. I cannot tell you how many times I've reviewed résumés of excellent physicians where one résumé read exactly like the rest. Who wants to hire an average leader when they can hire an exceptional, proven leader?

The formatting of your résumé is important! You want a document that's easy on the eyes, although obviously, the actual content is more important than the formatting. The following acronyms can help you frame your exceptional value:

CAR: context-action-result
SAR: situation-action-result
STAR: situation/task-action-result
PAR: problem-action-result

They essentially all represent the same concept: clearly link your value to the position you're applying for. Start by identifying a problem or situation you've already solved = context, situation, or problem. Next, list the actions you took to solve the problem and then state the result. Including a financial or other objective measure of the result adds impact as it affixes real-life measurable outcomes. Try to avoid the word "we" when describing actions taken, as the hiring manager is looking at *your* abilities. You can still convey a collaborative leadership style while taking credit for your actions. The following are a few examples:

> *There was a problem of inadequate staffing coverage. I devised a new staffing pattern that yielded a higher quality of care for patients and a better work-life balance for the providers, and obtained a cost savings of $350K annually.*

> *We had a resource-intensive, high-cost orientation program that wasn't scalable for company growth. I redesigned the orientation program, and that resulted in faster time to competency in a role by objective measures. This resulted in a cost savings of $3,850 per new hire, saving $1.1 million in just the first year.*

> *Our hospital was unable to maintain adequate staffing of ultrasound technicians due to night calls. I developed a protocol that instituted bridge medical therapy: having the patient return for their study the following day, utilizing*

first-morning appointments seven days a week. The result was a 95% decrease in night ultrasound studies, a decreased turnover rate of 87%, no negative patient outcomes, and a $45K savings annually in overtime pay.

Having degrees and letters after your name may help you find that next job but having the experience these CAR stories demonstrate is proof of value, and that value brings exponential worth. You need to prove your value through past accomplishments, regardless of the letters following your name. Refer to the chapter "Is MD or DO After Your Name Enough?"

When relating a CAR story, be concise. You spent ample amounts of time on a project, so it is not surprising that you want to share every detail. Let the interviewer ask you questions later if they are intrigued and need further clarification. The CAR story is a teaser to whet their appetite, progressing you through the initial screening process to the interview.

These CAR stories double as prep for an interview. You'll often be asked to provide an example of your expertise during an interview, and with these stories at your fingertips, you'll be well-prepared. Even if you're not directly asked, it's great to work these stories into your responses to questions. Choose your words wisely to clearly express that you're an action-oriented person who gets results while being collaborative and respecting other team members.

I cannot emphasize enough the need to enlist a professional résumé writer! You may believe that you're competent enough to write your own résumé and that may indeed be the case, but in my experience, a professional résumé writer, as their title implies, has specialized expertise in this area. Just as my hair stylist doesn't tell me how to practice medicine, I don't tell her how to do her job effectively. We can question each other to gain a greater understanding of a situation, but I don't pretend to hold expertise in someone else's area of specialty.

LinkedIn

A résumé writer may be able to help you design your LinkedIn page, too, and LinkedIn is a primary avenue for recruiters to find candidates. As a basic member of LinkedIn, you can explore (at no cost) the profiles of other individuals and companies just as they will review your profile. When I am interested in learning about a company, I always research the company and its leadership using LinkedIn profiles. I look at the employment history of the person who will be interviewing me. I explore where they lived and went to school, looking for commonalities. I use this information during the interview if the time is right. It is a sure bet they *will* review your profile before an interview.

LinkedIn is more of a business relationship form of social media, facilitating your ability to stay abreast of developments and advancements. It is a type of leadership development with a twist. LinkedIn allows you to build a network with whom you can stay in contact through the site's messaging tool. Recently, someone in my network reached out to me for advice based on my past employment. I answered his questions and, in turn, asked some of my own regarding his current organization.

There are numerous LinkedIn subscriptions beyond the basic, no-cost, option. LinkedIn Premium Career subscription allows you to see who has viewed your profile. Connecting with that individual can be a valuable networking resource. This option provides access to LinkedIn Learning, which covers a vast variety of topics from leadership development to skills such as Microsoft Excel. You can take proficiency exams, which allow for confirmation of your competencies. The premium subscription allows you to message an individual at the time you send a connect request. This can be very valuable as you can express your intent for connecting up front, increasing your chances of making a connection.

Perhaps one of the most valuable resources is job postings. You can place an "open to work" indicator on your profile, just as others may have a "hiring" indicator. After completing a profile, you will receive a regular listing of job opportunities matching your profile. There are links for easy applications.

I do not profess to be an expert in LinkedIn, but I can attest to it being a valuable resource. Explore the options yourself, as they do change over time. Determine if the added cost of the Premium or other subscription options is right for you. At a minimum, maintain a LinkedIn profile that is professional and always up to date.

Establishing Boundaries

It's critical to define your boundaries when contemplating new roles. An analogy would be buying a new home. You determine what the house *must* have and what you would *like* the house to have. Let's say you know you need a ranch model, at least three bedrooms, two bathrooms, an office, an attached two-car garage, and a specific school district. You would *like* to have four bedrooms and an additional half-bath plus a three-car garage. You're willing to consider one other school district, but the house must be a ranch, as one of the occupants is unable to climb stairs.

As you search for the perfect home, you know you won't look at any homes that have stairs — that's nonnegotiable. You won't settle for a home with fewer than three bedrooms, but you will consider one with five bedrooms in the other acceptable school district if the house otherwise meets your criteria. This same type of "must have/would like to have" list is applicable when considering your career move. Once again, be honest with yourself when you make your list! As an example, my list is as follows:

Must-haves:
- I need to believe in the mission. I need to drink the Kool-Aid.
- The patient is the North Star.
- The company has a positive, supportive, collaborative culture.
- It's a private equity, venture-capital-backed, or publicly traded company.
- There's an equity opportunity.

Preferences:
- I prefer a startup company or one that's in a growth phase, but I'm also willing to explore opportunities at later-stage companies.
- I prefer a company with a five-year endpoint plan, but I'm willing to explore opportunities where this endpoint is in less or more time.

- I prefer value-based care models.

Nonnegotiable:

- I will not relocate. I am willing to travel weekly.
- I don't want to work in a healthcare system/academic facility.

My list significantly simplifies my options when I research opportunities or when a recruiter reaches out to me with an opportunity to explore. I value my time while respecting the time of others! The entire process of seeking a new position can be daunting, especially if the opportunity you desire isn't immediately presented to you. Why should you interview for a position that doesn't align with your list? Doesn't align with your values? Doesn't align with your personality? Why should you compromise? Maybe you need a short-term compromise for a limitation that you cannot remove at this juncture in your career. Do not justify taking a position out of desperation or fear of not finding a better option unless you have a barrier you cannot modify. Ultimately, you will not be satisfied once you get settled into the new role.

This takes me to the next concept as you decide what's right for you. One of my former CEOs, an individual who highly valued people and served as a mentor to many, would tell me, "Make sure you run *to* something and not *away* from something." You may not be satisfied in your present job, but that's not a reason to compromise and accept a new position that you don't genuinely desire or that doesn't meet your needs. By running away from something, you'll likely be in the same place in the near future: unsatisfied with your job. Worse, your employer may not be satisfied with your performance, making a positive recommendation for your next opportunity unlikely.

Do *not* apply for a position before you have a résumé ready to upload and an updated LinkedIn profile. Once you apply, you'll be asked for your résumé if it hasn't already been requested, and you only have one opportunity to make a first impression. Scrambling to put together a subpar résumé or having a potential employer review a poorly structured or not-updated LinkedIn profile displays your lack of preparedness and organization. Is that the first impression you want to make with a potential employer? I suspect not.

You may want to modify your résumé for a given position, highlighting traits valued by a specific company. Occasionally, you will be asked to submit or have an opportunity to include a cover letter. Read the job description thoroughly so you can emphasize why you are the right candidate for the job. It is essential that your cover letter helps you stand out from other applicants. It is a daunting task for a recruiter to wade through application after application, choosing the right candidate to move on to the next step.

Do respond in a positive tone to any correspondence sent to you after your application and/or interview, even if it is a rejection. You never know when a position in the same company will be available as a perfect match for you. Your file will be reviewed, and that positive prior reaction will sit well with the recruiter, aligning you as a cultural fit. We discuss these concepts further in the chapter "Rough Waters."

You may be a lucky (or unlucky) person who gets tapped on the shoulder and invited to take on a new role. You're lucky if it's the role you've already identified as being your next step in your career journey. You're lucky if your skill sets match the role or if you have the wherewithal to develop the requisite skills. You're lucky if you have the support systems in place for your success. You are *un*lucky if you say yes because you're excited and honored to be offered this new shiny position, but you do so without first considering how this job aligns with your values, skills, must-haves, and non-negotiables list, and you.

Too often in medicine, especially entry-level leadership positions, a physician is offered a leadership role because they're next in line based on longevity. Other times, a promotion is offered because a person is good at their job. Excelling in a present role does *not* equate to having the skills needed in your next position. The next role often entails some degree of leadership advancement, although not always. Let me emphasize the necessity of *not* accepting an offer that's too good to be true before you've taken time to digest the big picture!

I learned during my MBA capstone that one of the most significant reasons for contract failures as a third-party vendor/partner with other companies directly correlates to inadequately armed medical directors. The company's medical directors were often promoted as "next in line" following the turnover of the prior medical director.

You may recall earlier I told a story of not believing I was the best physician in the department, which, at that point in my career, translated in my mind to not being the best candidate for medical director. Each of these roles, bedside physician and medical director, is associated with a different set of skills to optimize effectiveness. Being an excellent bedside physician did not equal being a stellar medical director. This identified medical director mismatch in bedside care versus leadership proficiency was combated from multiple directions, which included leadership development training, increased mentorship, improved standardized orientation programs of new medical directors, and a formalized screening of a candidate's aptitude to assume the medical director role.

Let's say you didn't receive a tap on the shoulder. Now what? Devise a plan to have the next door open for you. You're prepared — you already know what job you're pursuing. I've often asked when interviewing candidates, "Why do you want this particular role?" The answers have ranged from the candidate being aligned with the mission and values of the enterprise to the candidate being unhappy in their present job, and therefore, decided they'd apply for the role. Which candidate would *you* hire? When interviewing for a job, have conviction that fortifies your certainty toward the company and communicate it to the interviewer.

Engaging Your Network

Your plan will vary based on the position you desire, of course: the more competitive the position, the more robust the blueprint you'll need. A highly respected individual providing a word-of-mouth referral for you holds great value. This is not an easy find for most people, however. You'll need to build these relationships! Make a list of people who know you and you believe would be willing to be advocates for you, then contact each of them. Let them know exactly why you are contacting them and request their assistance. Allow them to prepare their response. Take the opportunity during the meeting to ask the person for advice. This conveys your respect for the person and often yields a desire on their part to help you.

Follow up on these encounters with a timely thank-you. Recap your ask and attach pertinent information such as a résumé or LinkedIn link. You want to unburden this person as much as possible by giving them the data they need to assist you. Consider including some high-impact CAR stories in this follow-up communication. Don't assume that anyone knows your accomplishments as well as you do. Keep the communication concise; don't send a novel that won't be read.

Expand your network. Strategically focus on making new connections. Become engaged in associations, attend conferences and meetings, and participate in social media outreach. Remember that while making connections is great, earning the respect and trust of your connections will take time.

I'm not a salesperson for LinkedIn, but I am an advocate for the platform due to personal experience. It's designed to help you network and search for jobs. I've seen many companies go through financial downsizing that required the termination of many employees, including over 100 physicians on one day. Posting and networking on LinkedIn quickly connected many of those laid-off individuals with new employment.

Recruiting Companies

Recruiters may help you make a match, but the ball is in your court to determine if it's the *right* match. I'm not implying that the engagement of a recruiter is ill-advised; effective recruiters are looking for a win-win situation, and in this scenario, the client and the candidate will have a great, long-lasting relationship. Recruiting firms want repeat business, so a less-than-ideal hire doesn't benefit them.

Interview Prep

The plan that you have when an opportunity arises directs the next phase of this journey. Nerves can get the best of you during an interview, and how you channel that energy is important. Consider hiring an interview coach to help maximize your strengths. You may be asked to give a presentation or be involved in a multi-person interview, and these scenarios may be a new experience for you. Embrace the experience and learn from each opportunity! Recruiters external to the company can prep you for an interview by sharing additional company or job information.

A good interviewer will ask if you have any questions for them at the end of the interview, so always have some questions prepared. Take this time to express what differentiates you from other candidates if you didn't have the chance to do so earlier in the interview. One question I often ask interviewers is, "Is there anything you've heard or seen during or before this interview that concerns you with respect to offering me this position? I would like to have the opportunity to ensure you have all the relevant information you need and an accurate perception of me when you're making your decision."

DO YOUR HOMEWORK. I rarely use the words never or always. This is one scenario where I can confidently state that you should *never* go into any interview unprepared. Learn as much as you can about the organization or company. Research how it started, their mission or purpose statement, vision, and values. Search the company on LinkedIn to read about their recent accomplishments and celebrations.

Make a list of the leadership team and anyone with whom you may work closely in the role for which you are interviewing. Review their LinkedIn profile. If you have a commonality with one of these individuals, mentioning it during the interview often makes a positive impact. Congratulating the company on a recent accomplishment shows that you are aligned with the company, engaged, and care about their mission. The person with whom you are interviewing feels valued.

You should receive a job description for the position to which you are applying. The job description serves many purposes, including aligning you as a good fit. Does the job description awaken your passion to go to work every day? Do you have questions about the job description to add to your interview question list? Is there any information you should add or subtract from your résumé to customize it for this opportunity? Are there buzzwords you should use during your interview or add to your post-interview thank-you communication?

Just as there are executive coaches and professional résumé writers, there are professional services to help you prepare for interviews. These interview coaches allow you to practice interviewing and provide feedback, helping you stand out from other candidates. When interviewing for a specific job, the coaches will help you prepare for anticipated questions you may be asked during the interview itself. At a minimum, you need to anticipate questions you will be asked and practice your presentation skills if you opt not to engage an interview coach.

A Virtual Interview Prep

Many of the recommendations that follow are related to virtual interviews; however, some apply to in-person interviews as well. Sometimes, sending a message through LinkedIn or via email in advance of an interview is appropriate. For example, if you have not yet shared your résumé, you can send it to the interviewer with a note expressing that you are excited to meet with them on (insert date) to explore (the specific opportunity). You can add a sentence regarding how you can add value to the company or how you stand out from other candidates. I prefer to use LinkedIn if I message someone in advance, as I believe it is more professional and less intrusive on their personal space.

Prior to the virtual interview, take time to prepare. Ensure you will have no distractions during the interview. Ask someone else to be responsible for tending the pets, children, and the door while you are being interviewed. Silence your phone. Dress professionally. It may be acceptable to wear athletic clothing during routine meetings at your organization, but this is not a routine meeting. Dressing professionally demonstrates respect for the person who is interviewing you, as well as for the position itself.

Check your technology. Make sure you have good connectivity. What will the interviewer see besides you? Do you need to clear the space on your desk? Add a background to your Zoom, Teams, or other platform? I once interviewed a candidate who had a beer can on their desk. As they were clicking out of the meeting, this person took a long swig of the beer.

Test your screen appearance before the interview. One way to do so is by sending yourself a "test" meeting invite on the same platform in advance. You can familiarize yourself with the meeting controls, such as the volume, mute, and camera buttons. Confirm that you will be centered on the screen without cutting off the top of your head. Position your laptop or tablet so you are not looking down; rather, you should be making eye contact with the interviewer as if you were in the same room. I often place two thick books under my laptop so I am not looking down.

Interview

Meeting Flow

Enter the meeting roughly five minutes before the meeting commences. Joining the meeting early allows time to troubleshoot any unforeseen connectivity issues. If this is an in-person interview, arriving early allows time to park and locate the interview room. Consider using the restroom prior to the interview.

ALWAYS be professional, no matter how well you know someone. However, you don't want to give the perception that you are distant or cold. You can mitigate this by your body language: smile, share commonalities you learned in your research, or congratulate the interviewer on a recent accomplishment you discovered while doing your homework. Avoid fidgeting. Smile and lean forward toward the camera or interviewer as this body language shows interest. Do not cross your arms.

Monitor the flow of the interview for the right time to interject CAR stories if you are not asked directly to provide an example. You can conclude your interview with a CAR story or two if you did not find any opportunity to sell yourself earlier. In your CAR stories, be cognizant that using "I" implies you are not a team player but using "we" implies you were not the leader. Make it clear that the outcomes are due to your leadership of a collaborative cross-functional team. Let the interviewer lead the discussion. Be concise in your answers while expressing the details of your CAR stories. The interviewer can ask additional questions to expand or better understand your answers. Being too wordy often leaves a negative impression. You want to ensure there is adequate time for an interviewer to dive deep into their areas of interest. If you spend excessive amounts of time answering a single question, you limit your opportunity to fully sell yourself.

What if you are asked to provide an example where you do not have experience? Do not sell goods you don't have! If you don't have experience in a particular area, be honest; if you have the wherewithal and the ability to learn a skill, say so. You need to build trust, and boasting about a skill you don't have will not work in your favor. You can reinforce being a phenomenal cultural fit with a proven successful track record in prior accountabilities and your confidence in learning the desired skills to excel at delivering desired outcomes. A great hiring manager will recognize that a plug-and-play new team member may provide fewer benefits than one who may need some short-term mentoring.

The types of questions you ask will vary based on the role for which you are interviewing. You may ask logistical questions like the length of a shift, how many shifts per week or month are expected, and the like. Glass Door or other reviews may raise some questions you want answered but be skeptical of what you read. Often, posts are made by dissatisfied employees for various reasons, similar to how patient reviews are submitted when someone is upset with their care or with a factor unrelated to their care. You may ask about the turnover rate in the company versus the national standard for a similar company, or what are the most frequent reasons expressed for leaving the company.

For higher-level administrative positions, a question such as "What keeps you awake at night?" can be revealing. You may ask about the five-year strategic goals and the plan to accomplish these goals. More specific roles will encounter more focused questions. AI is a great resource for suggesting questions you might be asked or ones you should ask yourself.

A good interviewer will leave time for questions. If they do not, you can request additional time now or in a future meeting to inquire further. Ensure that at some point in the process, all your questions have been answered prior to accepting an offer.

If anything you hear does not align with your goals, keep it to yourself unless you have no doubt you would decline an offer. Should that be the case, frame the statement positively. For example, you might say, "Thank you so much for your time, allowing us to explore this opportunity further. I do not believe this is the right match for me, as I cannot commit to the degree of travel required to be successful in the position. I firmly believe in the mission and culture of your company. I will continue to review your job board for positions that better align with me to bring positive value to the company."

Also, realize that your interview is not just the 30-, 45-, or 60-minute conversation you have with the interviewer. It includes anything you post on social media or outside discussions of your behavior. A health system CEO shared during a conference presentation that he was about to offer a position to an individual he was very excited to have join the team. Prior to making the offer, he overheard a restroom conversation during which the candidate was discussing the partying he had done the night prior and how poorly he felt that morning. Needless to say, he was not offered the position. Every interaction you have is a part of an interview process.

Salary Discussions

When is the right time to discuss salary? Ask a dozen people and you will likely get a dozen answers. Unfortunately, too many online applications request that you input a salary expectation. I prefer to hold that card in my hand until I learn the salary range being offered. If there is a significant difference, determine if the gap is unacceptable after weighing the benefits of the position should it be offered to you.

After a discussion to explore if they will compromise, respectfully decline if that gap is greater than you are willing to accept. A good rule of thumb is that the higher the level of leadership position you are contemplating, the earlier a salary range discussion will occur. You do not want to lead with a salary discussion, just as you do not want to waste your time or the hiring manager's and their team's time if you are so far apart in expectations.

This decision is significantly harder if you do not have a deep understanding of the role. You may opt to accept a lower salary to get your foot in the door with a new company or in a role where you are less experienced. When the interviewer inquires about my salary requirements, I ask about the budgeted salary range once we are further down the road, before sharing my desired salary. You may be pleasantly surprised to discover that their range is above your expectations. Therefore, I try to avoid any salary discussion early in the process.

Are there exceptions to that rule? Of course! I have had third-party recruiting firms meet with me for a screening interview. During this process, we explore if the position is well-suited for all parties. It may include a general salary discussion. If the recruiter believes we are so far apart that a company will not negotiate, we should not continue, as it would waste the time of all parties involved.

Consider all components of a salary and not just a base salary. What benefits are being offered? How do these benefits stack up against your present situation? Is there an option to request additional vacation time, bonus, or equity in exchange for a larger base salary? This is especially true in start-up companies, where money is not flowing as it would in a highly developed company with longevity.

If you are joining a larger healthcare system or company, there is often little room to negotiate. Contracts offered are a take-it-or-leave-it decision. It never hurts to inquire about the aforementioned compensation adjustments. You may have greater success with one-time costs such as a sign-on bonus or relocation fees. Loan repayments are an additional opportunity. Regardless, I recommend having a contract lawyer review the details to ensure you are certain of the terms of employment. No one can promise you a promotion if the company expands or if a vacant position is anticipated in the future. A total compensation package is more than salary, benefits, bonus, possibly equity, personal time off, and the like. I suggest you consider total compensation to include emotional equity.

Let me explain. I was in a ride-share vehicle one evening and asked the driver how he arrived in Boston. He told a story about having a great job in Miami when, to his total surprise, he was terminated. The job was reposted with the same job description and a lower salary to which he could apply. He instead opted to move to Boston and enjoy gainful employment as a ride-share driver. He explained that the emotional equity of his present job had significantly greater value than his previous employment, where, previously, he enjoyed working every day and always received great reviews. He no longer felt valued at his prior place of employment. If you have arrived at the point of contract negotiation, you likely have the emotional equity you desire.

Additional Interview Tips and Tricks

In-person interviews start as soon as you enter the parking lot. Any interaction with an employee prior to or following the interview can be shared with the interviewer. A firm handshake to start introductions is recommended. You may be taken on a tour of the facility. How you interact with people on this tour will get noticed. Avoid making negative comments about past employers. Express confidence. Conclude with a statement thanking your interviewer and the value you bring, differentiating yourself from others.

Remember, an interview is a two-way street. You are learning about the position to include expectations, culture, and other details just as they are interviewing you. You need to evaluate if this is a great fit for you, just as they are assessing if you are right for them.

There are new interview structures emerging in the virtual world. One more commonly utilized interview does not involve an interviewer. These are usually screening interviews where you, as the interviewee, are recorded on a virtual platform. You are often given one question at a time. Each question has a designated amount of time for each recorded answer. You can perform as many retakes as needed until you are satisfied with your answer.

This process is an efficient way to screen multiple candidates, narrowing the selection pool to move forward. You may feel like this is not a "real" interview since it is just you and the camera on your device. I assure you, these interviews are very real. Take them seriously just as you would take an interactive interview with someone. Prep for the interview. Ensure you send a communication expressing gratitude and highlighting what differentiates you from other candidates following this interview.

How many interviews can you expect? That all depends on the position to which you are applying. You will likely start with an interview by the recruiter, followed by the hiring manager at a minimum. Take the interview with the recruiter as seriously as you would with the hiring manager. A high-level executive position will have a series of escalating interviews, group interviews, and onsite interviews.

The most comprehensive set of interviews will start when a third-party recruiting firm is engaged for an executive position. You will begin with a screening interview by a junior partner in the recruiting firm. The next step is an interview with a senior partner in the recruiting firm. If you continue to advance, you will be presented to the company's executive team involved in the search. They will request a series of interviews if they like the recruiter's presentation. From there, the path may vary among companies. They often include different members of the executive team, may include a group interview, and, if a private equity or venture capital is involved, the interviews will include at least one member of that team.

Post-Interview

Send a note of gratitude immediately following the interview. This note should be personalized to the interviewer and include details that differentiate you from other candidates. This communication should be in an executive summary form, meaning it should be as concise and as factual as possible.

If you're working with a recruiter from a third party, it's a sign of respect to communicate with the recruiter following the interview. They'll want to know your perceptions of the position and the interview. Does the opportunity still resonate with you as you continue to learn more about it through the interview process? What is your perception of how the interview went? Are there still unanswered questions you have about the company? This recruiter has regular meetings with their clients. Your continued communication with the recruiter benefits all parties involved.

Continuous evaluation of the opportunity following each step in the interview process is imperative. The hiring company is doing the same with respect to you. Do not continue the process if, at any point, you determine the opportunity is not one you want to explore further.

Last, if an opportunity doesn't end in an offer, ask for feedback, either through the recruiter or directly from the decision-maker. Frame the request as one for personal growth, *not* one of anger. Express your appreciation for the opportunity and feedback, and praise the company's mission. You may feel as if you failed, but you have not! You'll grow stronger as you learn more along the way. The future chapter, *Rough Waters,* will look at this scenario.

IN SUMMARY:

1. Develop your CAR (context-action-result) stories.
2. Hire a professional résumé writer. Consider having this person develop your LinkedIn profile as well.
3. Make your must-haves, preferences, and non-negotiable list.
4. Network, network, network!
5. Consider working with an interview coach.
6. Do your homework prior to an interview, learning about the company, including the history, mission, vision and values, the people, the leadership team, and your interviewer.
7. Prep your interview space and yourself, ensuring high professional standards.
8. Remember that you are always interviewing.
9. Share CAR stories, be confident and concise, and watch your body language during an interview.
10. Send post-interview communication to the interviewer expressing gratitude for the opportunity to interview, their time, and what differentiates you from other candidates.

Closing The Deal

EXHALE

You are almost across the finish line. You've been offered a job. What's next? First, have all your questions been answered throughout the interview process? If not, seek the answer to those questions. Is there a pit in your stomach, or are you excited to begin your new position? If there is a pit in your stomach, something is not sitting right. Do you recognize the etiology of this feeling? If not, go back to the second and third chapters of this book to analyze if this is truly the right fit for you or if you have some unrecognized apprehension.

Contract negotiations can be challenging. Larger companies and health systems often have fixed contracts that offer little to no room for negotiating finer details. However, you should inquire about basic options regardless of the company's size. These may include relocation fees, licensure costs, loan repayments, and signing bonuses. Some specialties might allow for negotiation of salary, vacation time, and other contract aspects.

As you consider your contract, it's important to understand your BATNA: best alternative to a negotiated agreement. This term was defined by William Ury and Roger Fisher in their book *Getting to Yes: Negotiating Agreement Without Giving In*. BATNA is the most advantageous alternative that a negotiating party can accept if negotiations fail. Each party determines its own BATNA.

A classic example is buying a car. How much are you willing to pay before deciding to go to a different dealership or opt for a different model? What price is too high for you to accept? The dealership's BATNA is how much they are willing to lower the price versus losing a potential sale. If there is overlap between what you are willing to pay and the price the dealership is willing to offer, the dealership will likely sell you a car. The deal is advantageous to both parties.

When considering your BATNA in contract negotiations, you need to determine what you are willing to accept and what the alternative is if that offer is not made. Can you live with your decision either way?

Bargaining entails both sides making concessions. Smaller practices or businesses may be better suited for bargaining because they have greater flexibility to provide equity in place of a higher base salary, include incentives, and allow some degree of ownership in exchange for something on your desired list. Holding firm to a position often ends in both sides digging in their heels without reaching a deal. If a deal is reached without both parties compromising, there could be animosity, causing you to start off on a bad foot. It is difficult to keep emotions out of a negotiation. Objectivity is golden. Ultimately, you want your negotiations to build trust and respect. Consider having your contract lawyer negotiate for you.

A good contract should detail all terms in writing. Do not rely on verbal agreements or handshakes. Both parties need . A solid contract should cover such items as malpractice insurance, travel costs, bonuses, retirement contributions, benefits, moonlighting opportunities, restrictive clauses, and termination grounds.

How can you determine what is fair and equitable compensation? Clinical compensation models vary. You may be able to access clinical salary norms through your specialty organization. Pay attention to the geographic element of compensation, which is based on the cost of living for a given city or region. As a general rule, salaries are often higher in cities and lower in more rural settings despite supply and demand factors.

Contracts vary by position. A hospitalist's contract will differ from that of a CEO. Have a specialized contract lawyer review the contract with you to ensure clarity on the details. Some commonalities do exist or will be present in most contracts.

Base salary compensation is the most basic line item. Details regarding relative value units, reimbursement, or volume in fee-for-service contracts need to be understood in advance. Each year, the Centers for Medicare and Medicaid Services, CMS, determines the worth of an RVU. The average RVU reimbursement in 2024 was projected to be $32.74, reflecting a decrease of 3.4% from 2023. In 2025, there is an additional decrease of 2.8% or $32.3465 per

RVU. Services provided are weighted with specific RVU amounts. wRVUs, known as work RVUs, consider the physician's time, skill, and effort needed to deliver each service. wRVUs serve as a measure of a physician's productivity.

You may have a gating metric in your contract, meaning a minimal expectation of wRVUs required to meet minimal performance expectations. The contract will outline the penalties for not meeting minimal standards, if a minimal standard is set, and, on the other end of the spectrum, reimbursements for generating more than expected wRVUs.

For example, you may have a guaranteed base salary. You will get a specific reimbursement rate for each wRVU generated. Once you reach an upper threshold, the contract should dictate that wRVUs generated above the threshold are paid out at a lower, the same, or a higher rate. You need to know if being a high performer rewards you financially and make decisions based on these facts. Understanding that each person has individual performance outcomes that impact financial compensation, it is helpful to understand the median and salary range of other team members. This understanding will anchor your expectations within a reasonable span. Specific salaries of others will not be shared, but they may be willing to reveal the range.

Included in compensation is the amount of paid personal time off (PTO), also known as vacation days. Are you rewarded with time and separate financial resources for continuing medical education (CME)? Are there restrictions for using CME dollars, such as within the continental United States or for given subject matters? How is sick call handled? Does the company cover your license and DEA fees? You should inquire about relocation funding, if applicable. Signing bonus should be another area of inquiry, especially if you are applying for a difficult-to-fill position. The same reasoning should be applied to loan repayments. You may be required to commit to a dedicated length of time in the role to which you sign a contract in exchange for a relocation, signing, or loan repayment stipend(s).

In value-based care contracts, you will want to know the expectations for performance in relation to salary. In this world, there may be incentives for meeting quality metrics, achieving patient satisfaction, or working additional hours.

Compensation packages include benefits: retirement, health and other insurance options, bonus opportunities, equity, and other factors outside of the base pay. Understanding the offerings helps you compare multiple opportunities and also avoid unnecessary surprises down the road. The amount of malpractice coverage while employed and tail coverage following your departure should be spelled out.

Another category encompasses scheduled or non-direct patient care activities performed independently. These may include expected attendance at meetings, administrative duties, or responsibilities to enter into collaborative practice agreements with nurse practitioners or physician assistants. Details regarding on-call or holiday work should be included, along with information on how changes to these expectations are managed post-contract.

Additional details include the number of days and hours per week required, as well as weekend expectations. For instance, you might be expected to work four 10-hour days per week, inclusive of one weekend per month. If you have a hybrid role, it is important to ascertain how many hours are conducted in person versus remotely. If selecting a telehealth role, the contract should detail what equipment you must supply versus what the employer provides.

Your contract may require adherence to company policies and procedures or medical staff bylaws. Ask about any items that may cause friction. For example, requiring chart closures to include a discharge summary within seven days excluding vacation or FMLA time differs significantly from mandating completion within 24 hours of discharge regardless of your schedule. The next category addresses terms of termination. Often, contracts contain a "without cause" clause, indicating that termination can occur for no specific reason. You may be required to provide a specific number of days of advance notice before leaving the position. Consider this scenario: You receive an offer for a new opportunity that requires you to start within 30 days, but your current contract mandates 90 days' notice. Leaving on poor terms can hurt your future opportunities in the close-knit healthcare community. Discussing your departure with your current employer might yield an earlier release date or an amicable solution without negative downstream effects.

Termination clauses can include restrictive covenants limiting opportunities in similar roles within your new position. Although many states have legislation prohibiting such clauses, some still enforce these "no compete" clauses, creating significant controversy. Understanding the impact of restrictive covenants is crucial. Some contracts may limit your opportunity to recruit individuals following your departure.

Do not sign any contract without thoroughly understanding all its outlined details. Legal language can be complex and unfamiliar. I strongly recommend that you have a contract attorney review the terms before signing. Letters of intent might appear benign, but can contain binding details. *Hence, do not sign a letter of intent until reviewed by your contract attorney.*

Getting to the contracting stage is a gratifying part of the career journey. Safeguarding yourself by negotiating and having a detailed understanding of the contract is imperative.

IN SUMMARY:

1. Confirm your questions have been answered and you are confident the job you are about to negotiate a contract is the right option for you.
2. A contract lawyer will advocate for you, ensure you understand the nuances of your contract, and negotiate an optimal contract.
3. Understand your BATNA — best alternative to a negotiated agreement — to set boundaries during a contract negotiation.
4. Ensure your contract outlines all details to protect both yourself and the party with whom you are entering into an agreement.
5. Inquire about additional compensation package opportunities that may not be offered up front, such as relocation, signing bonus, or loan repayment reimbursement.

Rough Waters

DEEP BREATH

It would be awesome if every day could go as planned, but that's not reality. You still get put on hold, your inbox is rarely empty, and not every project is finished on time. The same is true in your career. You may approach a new opportunity knowing you are fully qualified. You have objective evidence to support your confidence. You are taken aback when you are not even granted an interview. You must face the fact that you were NOT chosen. Most people's minds immediately turn to themselves, suspecting they did something wrong along the way. Others become angry at the hiring manager for not recognizing a great "thing" that was right in front of them. There are many reasons for this situation to unfold.

I like to break these potential reasons for not getting an offer into two buckets. The first bucket is items you potentially can influence for future experiences. The second bucket is items out of your control. These buckets are not an exhaustive list as they include the more commonly experienced responses.

Bucket 1: Factors You May Be Able to Influence

Resume Screening Process

ISSUE: When applying for a position in today's world, larger companies or positions that attract hundreds or more applicants may use artificial intelligence (AI) to screen resumes. AI is looking for certain key words in a résumé. Résumés are "disqualified" from advancing in the process if they are missing these key items; those that include these key words are advanced for further screening. It isn't easy to know what the buzzwords are. A friend of mine was told she was "not qualified" when she requested feedback as to why she was not granted an interview. Months later, the position was still not filled. A friend of this individual mentioned her name to the CEO of the company, whose recruiter rejected her, endorsing her qualifications.

The CEO was unaware that she had been rejected from the start, and immediately interviewed her, as did multiple other executives in the company. She received a job offer.

At present, AI is not commonly used to screen executive-level positions. These positions are highly specialized, gaining the stature of personalized screenings. How AI affects these positions in the future is yet to be seen.

POTENTIAL SOLUTIONS: Not everyone has a friend with the ear of the hiring manager. Study the job description, specifically the qualifications for that role. Adapt your résumé to include these qualifications if they are indeed skills you possess. Do not claim expertise you do not have, as this will be discovered quickly, undermining your character.

Next, research the name of the hiring manager. Scan the job description for an indication of who the role reports to. You may need to call the recruiter or the department and inquire who the role reports to. Then construct a concise, well-written message as to why you are applying, what differentiates you from other applicants, and request an opportunity to speak further. Attach your résumé to the message and email it to the hiring manager.

You can often determine the hiring manager's possible email address by looking at other email addresses in the company. LinkedIn messaging is an alternative. You can message the recruiter if you cannot identify the hiring manager. Even if you don't get a direct response, your enthusiasm for the job will be noted.

Required Skills Sets

ISSUE: You would not hire an electrician for a plumbing job just as you would not hire an orthopedist to perform cardiothoracic surgery. Consider a job that requires proficiency in point-of-care ultrasound (POCUS). You have ample experience with proven outcomes in all other requirements for the job, but you are not skilled in POCUS. Is POCUS the dominant skill set required, or is it a small percentage? Is there an opportunity to cover this small gap in another way until you become proficient in POCUS? Or, is POCUS a skill you have no desire to acquire, so you choose to pass on this opportunity?

POTENTIAL SOLUTIONS: The obvious solution is to acquire this skill set, especially if you see it as a requirement for most future positions that interest you. Since you cannot snap your fingers and have these abilities automatically, it may take some time before you can start applying for these options. You can develop a plan to acquire the desired skill, demonstrating your commitment to rounding out your abilities. This may be a viable option for you to apply for one of these positions today. I would not take this route if a large fraction of the role requires this skill.

Next, look at the job requirements. Does it state the competency is preferred versus required? Preferred offers some flexibility, especially if you have already developed a plan to learn the skill set. An additional option is to look at the big picture. There are times a job description may be written by an individual who does not fully understand the role's requirements or may be less experienced at writing job descriptions. Do not be so presumptuous as to assume you know the role better than the person who is responsible for the posting.

Be inquisitive, as you may be able to find an alternative solution to this dilemma. A word of caution: Be truthful during your interview. Do not try to gloss over or exaggerate your abilities. You may recall in the chapter "Imposter Syndrome," I spoke about a preference to hire someone with the wherewithal to learn a skill who will complement the team and culture over someone who is plug-and-play ready with potential negative or less future positive impacts. YOU could be this person with the wherewithal that the hiring manager is determined to place on their team.

Proven Track Record

ISSUE: Terms like "consistently delivers" or "achieved desired outcomes" are great for the worker bee employees we discussed previously. An employee wants their worker bees to be dependable, including someone who consistently delivers on key performance indicators (KPIs). Leadership positions often demand more than someone who "meets" expectations. Leaders should "exceed" expectations. Companies will seek individuals with proven results that meet their needs, meaning a small positive impact project will not suffice for a large multi-hospital healthcare system or national company.

POTENTIAL SOLUTIONS: The most effective way to overcome the lack of a proven track record is to have objective evidence of your accomplishments *and* ensure you are communicating the results effectively. Adding a dollar amount to the impact you have created elevates your application. Make your CAR stories vibrant. You do not want your résumé to read like those of most candidates, as that will not project why you are a preferred candidate over others. Use verbs that convey excitement when describing your actions. If you are not provided an opportunity to prove yourself and do not have the desired proven track record, take a step back to gain this experience. You may ask a mentor or your direct supervisor if you can assume a larger project under the mentorship of a proven, successful leader, thus enhancing your CAR stories.

Ageism

ISSUE: The Age Discrimination Employment Act (ADEA) considers anyone over 40 years old to be legally protected from ageism. That is mid-career for many individuals, a time of job advancement and growth. It is illegal to ask for someone's age during the interview process; however, your résumé with graduation dates will provide clues to the interviewer.

So why would there be bias against a more experienced physician? The bias may stem from unjustified beliefs that older individuals are not up to date on the latest technologies, or that they are slower and less productive, that they are less open to change because they are set in their ways. Younger, less experienced leadership physicians may be hired over the older, more experienced physicians because their salary demands are lower. This thought process can be very near-sighted. Yes, the younger physician may cost less on paper, but the ROI may be a fraction of that of the older, more experienced physician.

POTENTIAL SOLUTIONS: What can you do to combat ageism? It is important that you exhibit energy and enthusiasm during your interview. During the interview, lean forward or into the camera if this is a virtual interview, tell your CAR stories, and how you want to replicate their success exponentially for the role to which you are applying. Articulate how change energizes you, stimulates you for future progress, and how you ease the strain of change management within your teams. If there is new technology in the field to which you are applying, and you are proficient with this technology, do not hide that fact. Make certain you are clear and deliberate in communicating it to the interviewer. Do not assume that they know your capabilities.

Bucket 2: Factors You May Be Unable to Influence

Budget Restraints

Budgets are frequently set more than a year in advance. Business performance may change, just as reimbursement rates for clinical care are not constant year over year. Your skills may be severely needed. If there is no money in the budget, an employer's hands may be tied.

An employer may be able to get creative with the finances to remain budget neutral, provided they can sustain the costs year-over-year. An employer may reallocate dollars to a new position and eliminate a present vacant position. There may be a freeze on vacant positions, limiting reallocation of these funds. They may need to cut expenses elsewhere to augment your hire. An example may be to change an onsite meeting to a virtual meeting. There is a risk to the hiring manager: the finance team may request to retain these cost reductions in the following year's budget, even if it does not benefit the team.

Being aware of budget issues may allow you to get creative if you are willing to make sacrifices and accept some risk. You may offer a reimbursement schedule based on an objective ROI measurement. Let's say you are applying for a position in a new wound care program yet to be launched. Equipment is already in place. You determine the cost per patient to provide services. You ascertain the reimbursement rates to care for an average patient. You agree to take a percentage of the profit for each patient cared for in the new wound care program up to a salary cap amount, allowing a margin to cover overhead expenses.

This places a burden on you to grow the program. It places a risk in that your salary may not meet your expectations initially or at all if the program does not flourish. On the flip side, if the program exceeds expectations under your leadership, you will be tapped on the shoulder for the next project and can demand a higher reward up front.

An alternative option may be to serve as a consultant. Both parties get to know each other better, and if the relationship is a good fit, consulting could lead to a full-time position ... or nothing. Again, risks are inherent to this approach. Benefits will not be provided. Determine your BATNA and whether these options are the right course for you.

Predetermined Hire Prior To Job Posting

Most companies require a job posting for 72 hours before an offer. There are many cases where the hire is identified before the job posting. This person could be an acquaintance, often someone the hiring manager has worked with in the past. The decision may be to hire an internal candidate, and you are an external candidate. Jim Collins' book *Good To Great* cites promoting from within as a characteristic of great companies.

You may see this posting and apply for the position. There is no signage with flashing lights indicating that this door will remain closed to you. One option, which will not land you the job, is to reach out to the hiring manager on LinkedIn or through email. Introduce yourself, share your elevator pitch, and indicate you would like to be a member of their team in the future.

Multiple Qualified Candidates

You may do everything well throughout the interview process, but maybe someone with similar qualifications lives closer, so that person is chosen over you. They may be stronger in one skill set, while you are stronger in another. Their skill set fills a void on the team over your own. There are so many small variables that are out of your control. Do not beat yourself up. The right fit for you will happen at the right time.

Perceived Salary Requirements

A hiring manager may make assumptions about your salary requirements based on your prior roles or skill sets. You may provide a number. Someone else may provide a lower number. Two paths can transpire. The hiring manager may choose to hire the less expensive option without the forward thinking of the ROI each person brings to the table. For example, the lower salary demand person may have an ROI of double their salary, while you, the higher salary demand applicant, may provide a tenfold ROI. Clearly, the tenfold ROI is the better value. Nearsightedness on the hiring manager's part will cost them dearly.

If you are willing to accept a lower salary after determining your BATNA, make that fact known. I have been personally told I am overqualified. In my mind, the company is getting a bargain for its dollar. They are concerned I will leave when I find something better. They do not know me and my intentions when I enter a contract where the company's mission and my values are all aligned.

Geography

You may or may not be willing to relocate. Regardless, a company that wants someone in a specific location is usually a non-negotiable for the hiring manager. You may be willing to relocate, which is great. If they need someone in the role yesterday and have another equally or even less-qualified candidate residing locally to the position, your willingness to relocate may not factor into their decision.

Reorganization

Reorganization is more common in early- to mid-stage companies and companies recently undergoing a merger or acquisition than in mature companies. On the contrary, this circumstance is a normal function of any company. Companies are always exploring how to be more efficient, how to manage growth or new entities affecting the business model. A company may pilot new programs that require a rework of current teams. Thinking through a proper organizational structure takes time. It is not unusual for a position to be posted or to proceed through interviews only to learn the company has opted to go a different direction.

The different direction can be based on several reasons. They may recognize that they want different qualifications in a candidate than they originally thought. They may determine that one hire can fill two open roles, or someone already established in the company can take on the added responsibility in the short term. They may divide the job responsibilities among multiple present employees.

This "different direction" can be a polite way for a recruiter to state you are not the right fit for the position. Do not assume the reorganization "excuse" is personal. Requesting feedback following a declination of your candidacy will reveal this information, provided the person offering the feedback is forthcoming. You can ask the question directly during the feedback session if you believe it is warranted.

Many other factors can affect why you were not the chosen applicant. Ask for feedback. Every interview is a learning process. The feedback may be hard to swallow. Fight getting defensive. Send a thank-you note following the conversation. Develop an action plan based on the feedback for factors you can modify. Maybe you do not interview well. Engage with an interview coach. This is not the easy part, and certainly is not pleasurable. The pot of gold at the end of the rainbow is more gratifying. I do not look at these situations as failure, despite how they make you feel. They are opportunities for growth. The key word being OPPORTUNITY.

As Robert F. Kennedy said, "Only those who dare to fail greatly can ever achieve greatly."

IN SUMMARY:

1. Not every journey will end with a job offer.
2. There are some factors you can influence in the search process, and others you cannot.
3. Every interview is an opportunity to gain personal experience and growth.

4. Request feedback and develop an action plan based on the feedback, should you not get an offer.
5. Develop an action plan from lessons learned.

Pitfalls to Avoid

HAZARDS

The process of changing or advancing a career is frequently the equivalent of its own full-time job. Self-exploration and discovery take time. Carrying out a plan to cover gaps in your knowledge and skills takes time. Having this change come at the right time in your life takes time. Having the stars align to network, be presented with the opportunity to interview, and be selected for a job offer — specifically, one that meets your expectations — takes time.

Time: Friend or Foe?

Time can often feel like an enemy. Most physicians have personalities that are always on the go. We must be efficient. We must work accurately and effectively, and quickly move to the next "thing" on our plates. The fee-for-service payment model encourages speed. Our plates are always full. But despite this natural inclination, you must respect that this process takes time, especially when you're making a significant change. I was not the woman who enjoyed her pregnancy, so waiting 40 weeks for our bundle of joy to be born was an eternity! Looking back, 40 weeks goes by so fast.

Hearing someone declare, "The right thing will happen at the right time" can be frustrating. And it's disappointing when the right opportunity does *not* present itself or someone else gets the offer you wanted. Just remember that time heals most wounds.

This process requires resiliency. Giving up will not get you across the finish line! When you're feeling overwhelmed, take a step back. Take time to reenergize. That may involve taking a vacation, stepping away from the search process for a limited amount of time, exercising, spending more time with family and friends, doing a puzzle or a lot of puzzles, reading a book through to the last page, or doing whatever fills your tank. Be "The Little Engine That Could."

Speaking with a mentor, coach, or objective individual can help you gain insights that might be difficult to gain on your own. You may be reaching for a rung on the ladder that's too high for your present skill set. You may need to start at a lower rung on the ladder, especially if you're climbing a new ladder. A bucket of experience in a clinical field will help, but it does not equate to a bucket of experience in administrative roles — while you were doing highly technical surgeries, you weren't gaining experience in people-management issues.

You may have set your sights on a goal that's not attainable today. However, it *is* attainable in your future! Many companies want you to grow within an organization to earn a higher-level position rather than step into it from the outside. Jim Collins' book *Good to Great* describes how the best performing companies promote from within. If that's the company's culture, no matter what you do, it is unlikely you will get to enter the company at that higher level. Your mentor or coach can be your cheerleader and lift your spirits when this scenario happens. You may be on the correct course, and your supporter(s) can reinforce your need for resiliency. They often have experience in this process, understanding that it takes time. It is easier for someone else to objectively evaluate the situation versus the individual who feels like they cannot escape the quicksand on which they are standing.

If you get worn down or feel discouraged, know that such feelings are normal. This process can deflate you. Many reasons for rejection will have nothing to do with you personally, as discussed in the prior chapter, "Rough Waters." Some reasons that I experienced were company leadership changes, the company acquiring another company, my strengths already being strengths within the company, and other candidates better rounding out the company's needs, the company deciding they wanted the candidate to relocate after all, etc.. Don't stumble by entering an interview *not* feeling energized and confident! Most people aren't good actors; if we were, we would be in a totally different career. You need to genuinely be at your best for every interview.

Assumptions

Let's talk about assumptions. Do *not* make any assumptions that your present manager knows your goals. Putting out signals, hinting, or — worse yet — not saying anything at all does not promote your needs. Don't be scared to ask for a meeting and express your goals. Develop a plan together to meet those goals. Of course, doing so doesn't guarantee a future opportunity; in fact, you cannot bluntly ask for a guaranteed opportunity.

But you *can* excel in your execution of the plan, and you *can* develop your personal brand and value story so that you're the candidate the others need to match up against. Managers are just as busy as you are, and knowing your aspirations is usually not their top priority. An executive physician colleague of mine shared several stories of people who told him their goals and people *who did not express* their goals. Would you like to hazard a guess as to who was more supported on their journey?

Only *you* can do the best job of selling *you*. *You* are the only one who's looking out for your best interests. Do not assume that a recruiter or anyone else is 100% in your court!

Also, do not assume that everyone wants to climb a ladder. In my case, my MBA program reenergized me. You're reading this book because you want to be empowered to advance or change your career. However, not everyone is interested in doing that. I realized this when I was mentoring one particular physician, who stated that he was happy coming to work each day, doing his shift, and then going home. I agreed that he was a physician who provided exceptional patient care. I could depend on him to always arrive at work on time, not create waves, and adapt quickly to any workflow changes. He was a satisfied worker bee, and who wouldn't want a team of dedicated worker bees?

Exceptional Résumé

A high-level executive physician affirmed the need for a professional résumé writer. This colleague was a highly accomplished physician leader who had applied for a job outside of our present company. The recruiter laughed at his résumé: The physician had listed his jobs and responsibilities, but didn't include any context-action-result stories. He didn't stand out on paper, even though the recruiter knew his worth. Imagine my colleague's embarrassment when he heard that the résumé he'd devised was viewed as a joke document!

Honesty

Back to pitfalls for you to avoid. Throughout this book, I've emphasized that you need to be honest with yourself. Don't allow yourself to be persuaded to have a given value or feel like you cannot go where you'll be happiest based on other people's values or comments. *You are your own person.* Don't feel ashamed, embarrassed, or deflated if you have values that aren't the "norm," so long as they don't hurt anyone else. Be honest when evaluating your strengths and gaps in proficiencies. Imposter syndrome can cause you to underestimate your strengths, while overconfidence will make you inflate your competencies.

Don't accept an offer or decline an offer for the wrong reasons. We've discussed how disparaging the process can be at different steps along the way. Failing to get a job offer after several interviews takes a negative toll on the psyche. On the other hand, it may be tempting to accept an offer that doesn't line up with your must-haves and non-negotiables. You might rationalize why signing an acceptance letter is the right decision. Maybe it is, but often it isn't. At the same time, don't let analysis paralysis stop you from signing an acceptance letter. Refer to the "What's Stopping You?" chapter if you find yourself conflicted about accepting an offer. Dig deep to determine why you are hesitant to sign, especially if the opportunity aligns with your values and desires.

One more scenario to consider: You have an offer that does indeed match your lists for the most part and everything about the position feels right... except the salary, bonus, and benefits. Your balloon feels like it just burst again. Maybe, but maybe not. Refer to the chapter "Closing the Deal." Consider your definitions of happiness and success. You must decide where to draw the line and how hard to push if the offer otherwise satisfies your definitions of happiness and success. Pushing too hard for more money or other financial aspects may push you out of a job; the employer may perceive that you care more about the money than the mission. How will you feel if you do not get the job? More importantly, how will you feel if you do get the position for a little less compensation but a whole lot more happiness? Money can help you meet basic needs. Money cannot buy happiness.

Putting It Together Checklist

FINALE

I cannot emphasize enough how much you need to be candid with yourself as you answer the following questions.

☐ Why do you want to make a career change?

_____

_____

_____

_____

☐ Is your desire to make a change for the right reasons? Is your rationale for change objective or an emotional reaction to a situation?

_____

_____

_____

_____

☐ Reflect on why you haven't made a change yet. What barriers do you need to overcome to make a change?

_____

_____

_____

_____

☐ What are your top 3–5 personal values? Why?

_____

_____

_____

_____

_____

_____

☐ Are you experiencing some degree of imposter syndrome? How can you overcome these self-imposed perceptions?

_____
_____
_____
_____
_____
_____
_____
_____

☐ What are your greatest strengths? Does your greatest strength equal your greatest weakness, and if so, how can you mitigate this weakness?

_____
_____
_____
_____

☐ What is your personality profile? For example, if using Myers-Briggs, you may be ISTJ.

_____
_____
_____
_____

☐ What career choices best match your personality profile? What career choices are likely an imprecise match for your personality?

_____
_____
_____
_____

☐ What is your optimal personal brand?

_____
_____
_____
_____

☐ How do others view your personal brand?

_____

_____

_____

_____

☐ How do you handle stressful situations or react when fatigued? What impact have these situations had on your personal brand?

_____

_____

_____

_____

☐ What are the qualities you experienced in a great preceptor (or mentor)? How can you become a better preceptor (or mentor)?

_____

_____

_____

_____

☐ What skills and experiences best match your present needs in a mentor?

_____

_____

_____

_____

☐ Who can you approach to mentor yourself?

_____

_____

_____

_____

☐ Why or why not is an executive coach an option for you to explore at this point in your career?

_____

_____

_____

_____

☐ What are your five- and 10-year SMART goals? Identify your one- and three-year SMART goals as a way to achieve your five- and 10-year goals.

In 10 Years:

S (Specific): _____

_____

M (Measurable): _____

_____

A (Achievable): _____

_____

R (Relevant): _____

_____

T (Timely): _____

_____

In 5 Years:

S (Specific): _____

_____

M (Measurable): _____

_____

A (Achievable): _____

_____

R (Relevant): _____

_____

T (Timely): _____

_____

In 3 Years:

S (Specific): _____

_____

M (Measurable): _____

_____

A (Achievable): _____

_____

R (Relevant): _____

_____

T (Timely): _____

_____

In 1 Year:
S (Specific): _____

M (Measurable): _____

A (Achievable): _____

R (Relevant): _____

T (Timely): _____

_____

☐ What is your plan to make your career goals known within your organization?

_____

_____

_____

_____

_____

☐ What is your definition of happiness?

_____

_____

_____

_____

_____

☐ What is your definition of success?

_____

_____

_____

_____

_____

☐ Identify how you work best: What is your ideal work environment, work structure, and work type?

_____

_____

_____

_____

☐ List your top 4–6 values in a work environment.

_____

_____

_____

_____

_____

_____

☐ What additional degrees, certifications or education will help you achieve your goals?

_____

_____

_____

_____

☐ Where do you have gaps? Do your short-term SMART goals include a plan to address these gaps?

_____

_____

_____

_____

☐ Identify your key stakeholders who will be affected by this change. Discuss your goals with and garner support from them.

_____

_____

_____

_____

IF YOU PLAN TO START YOUR OWN COMPANY, STOP HERE! DETERMINE YOUR BEST NEXT STEPS AND RESOURCES.

☐ Develop a minimum of three CAR stories for each of your last three jobs.

CAR #1/most recent job:

Context: _____

_____

_____

Action: _____

_____

_____

Result:_____

_____

_____

CAR #2/most recent job:

Context: _____

_____

_____

Action: _____

_____

_____

Result:_____

_____

_____

CAR #3/most recent job:

Context: _____

_____

_____

Action: _____

_____

_____

Result:_____

_____

_____

CAR #1/second-most-recent job:

Context: _____

_____

_____

Action: _____

_____

_____

Result:_____

_____

_____

CAR #2/second-most-recent job:

Context: _____

_____

_____

Action: _____

_____

_____

Result:_____

_____

_____

CAR #3/second-most-recent job:

Context: _____

_____

_____

Action: _____

_____

_____

Result:_____

_____

_____

CAR #1/third-most-recent job:

Context: _____

_____

_____

Action: _____

_____

_____

Result:_____

_____

_____

CAR #2/third-most-recent job:
Context: _____

_____

_____

Action: _____

_____

_____

Result:_____

_____

_____

CAR #3/third-most-recent job:
Context: _____

_____

_____

Action: _____

_____

_____

Result:_____

_____

_____

☐ Develop your résumé, preferably with a professional résumé writer. List names/contact info of potential résumé professionals.

_____

_____

_____

_____

☐ Develop or update your LinkedIn profile.

☐ What's on your must-haves list with respect to a new position?

_____

_____

_____

_____

☐ What's on your prefer-to-have list with respect to a new position?

_____

_____

_____

_____

☐ What's on your non-negotiable list?

_____

_____

_____

_____

☐ Establish a relationship with someone who can provide you with interview coaching. List their name and contact information.

_____

_____

_____

_____

☐ Identify networking individuals with whom you have established relationships. Contact these individuals in person if possible.

_____

_____

_____

_____

☐ Identify sources to expand your networking opportunities.

_____

_____

_____

_____

☐ Contact recruiters. List their names and contact information.

_____

_____

_____

_____

☐ Follow up on all contacts (people you met at networking events, recruiters, interviewers) with personalized thank-you notes.

_____

_____

_____

_____

☐ Prior to signing a contract, consider:
    ☐ Have all your questions been answered?
    ☐ Did a contract lawyer review and explain the contract to you?
    ☐ What is your BATNA?

_____

_____

_____

_____

☐ Obtain feedback throughout the interview process. Remain resilient!

☐ Sign the acceptance contract.

☐ Celebrate!

I believe you *can* achieve your career aspirations. Please share your stories with me on LinkedIn: www.linkedin.com/in/pamcorisullivan so we can celebrate together. Maybe I will feature your story in another book so you can be an inspiration to others.

Vignettes

IN THEIR WORDS

Determining your career path can be exhilarating, daunting, and any combination in between. Each decision will have upsides, downsides, risks, and benefits. Your goal is to land in a place with mostly upsides and benefits. There are times you may feel alone on the journey. You may question your choices. You are not isolated on an island.

While writing this book, I had a vision to share the stories of physicians from a variety of specialties, career paths, and stages in their careers in the hope that they will inspire and support you. **Every** physician has a story to tell, as few have had an easy career journey. I asked them to write about their decision-making processes, emotions, and anything important that they believe could benefit others. I did not provide parameters with regard to length, as everyone's story is different. I am so grateful to each of these physicians who took time from their busy lives to share themselves and their stories. I have learned from them, am inspired by them, and have shed a tear reading their struggles. I present their career stories in their own words.

In His Words: Jonathan D. Block, MD, MBA, MLS, MPH, CPE
https://www.linkedin.com/in/
jonathan-block-md-mba-mls-mph-cpe-7327269/

UNPLANNED JOURNEY

This is the story of my career in medicine, the paths taken and untaken. It's a meandering tale, not fraught with danger and action-packed adventure, but one that I am excited and also fearful to share. It's been said that every story should start at the beginning, but the problem here is trying to find "the beginning. "So, I will start as far back as I can without boring anyone to tears.

I can honestly say I remember little from my childhood except those sentinel events that mark key points in forming my behavior and my path. My father passed away when I was eight due to severe complications of his uncontrolled brittle diabetes. In those days, the mid to late 1970s, urine glucose strips were the best they had to monitor patients while offering him self-administered insulin with the glass and stainless-steel syringes I still keep as a memento.

Shortly thereafter, I knew I wanted to be a doctor. I went through elementary school knowing I wanted to go into medicine, even creating horrible, rudimentary anatomy drawings with incorrect markings just to pretend. There were a few times in high school when I questioned my choice, even though I excelled in the sciences and biology, in particular. I almost deviated into computer science, but once again, that "calling" tugged at the primitive hindbrain as an instinctual guide.

I double majored in college. First, I majored in general science as a typical pre-med student, and I also became an emergency medical technician, working both on my college campus and on an ambulance service on the outskirts of Boston for three years while school was in session. During this time, I became a phlebotomist at a hospital near my hometown, taking shifts when I was home on breaks and during the summer months.

I was studying philosophy as my second major, feeling that I most likely would be relegated to the sciences the rest of my working life, so why not enjoy learning something I wanted when I could. When given the choice of graduating with honors by completing a thesis in philosophy or an experimental project in the sciences, I prepared outlines for both options, but chose the thesis in philosophy in the area of the philosophy of religion.

I contemplated deviating from medicine altogether a few times in college. Once, I considered culinary school as I enjoyed cooking and found the kitchen my peace, and another few times, I considered abandoning medical school and going to rabbinical seminary to become a rabbi. It dawned on me that although cooking was a passion and the service aspect of being a rabbi tapped into some of my personal drives, neither was a true path for me. So, I resolved myself that medical school and becoming a physician was my calling and encompassed all my desires.

I should mention that while I was in college, I began my leadership journey, first as a resident adviser in the dorms during both my junior and senior years. I learned I was a horrible leader at the time. Despite some of the basics on how to address situations with the perfunctory three-day training sessions before the students arrived for the semester, I had a particularly difficult time deviating from the more authoritarian aspects of my personality. It was an eye-opening experience to see myself through the eyes of others, but I wasn't fully ready to embrace the "constructive criticism" just yet. Still, some of the words of my directors still linger in the back of my mind, and I will always be grateful to one of them in particular for his words that guide me to this day.

> *It was an eye-opening experience to see myself through the eyes of others, but I wasn't fully ready to embrace the "constructive criticism" just yet.*

I applied for medical school as we all did back then: requesting applications, filling them out on a typewriter, and writing my essays, being ever so careful not to overuse the whiteout for the obligatory mistakes college students make.

My essay was the standard "Why I want to become a physician." I wrote about my father's illness, the havoc it created for my family, leaving my mother to raise two sons without any real career skills to find meaningful work. That meant we subsisted on tight finances and had to forgo amenities most of my friends enjoyed as a routine.

My older sister was already out of the house by then, and the family dynamics after my father's death forced her estrangement. It was, to say the least, difficult, but it forged a very distinct personality trait of mine. Not only do I rise to it, but I do not give up in the face of a challenge, though my mother used to say I'd cut off my nose to spite my face. Thankfully, a lifetime of lessons has tempered that.

My essay touted how much I wanted to help those around me and fight diseases like diabetes with the goal of becoming an endocrinologist to prevent anyone else from having to suffer with the loss of a family member the way my brother and I had. I was accepted into a few schools, and was able to return to New York to attend SUNY Stony Brook, which saved me financially, as I was footing the bill myself.

The first two years of medical school were standard, with classes in anatomy, pathology, etc., making friends, some of whom I still stay in contact with, and some I regret not staying connected with. In my first two years of medical school, I worked as a medical technologist at the same hospital where I had been a phlebotomist. I had been training in the laboratory testing areas while in college, and to the chagrin of many of the techs and supervisors there, I became proficient and knowledgeable. Again, I faced a challenge — this time, workplace discrimination, which I never imagined would affect me.

Again, I faced a challenge — this time workplace discrimination, which I never imagined would affect me.

In New York at the time, there were two ways to become a medical technologist: graduate from an accredited four-year degree program or do a clinical training pathway with a bachelor's in a science field. I did the latter. I learned the areas of hematology, chemistry, and toxicology. I was the only one on the midnight shift (my preferred time so no one bothered me) to be able to run microbiology due to my medical school education and lab practicums, making me proficient at plating the patient specimens (i.e., blood, sputum, etc.) on the nutrient plates to place in the incubators.

I drew the attention of the lab manager in a bad way because I openly challenged some of the supervisors above me when, in my mind, they didn't understand pathophysiology and why results came out the way they did. I also gained the attention of the lab director, an older pathologist who invited me to join him on autopsies and learn a few things. I realized that special attention from the lab director created quite a bit of jealousy, and fueled by my sense of fairness, amplified the difficulty of me staying in the lab, but I persevered for the clinical experience and the paycheck. I stayed in the lab for the first two years of medical school, then worked a side job due to the time demands of entering the third year and clinical rotations.

I am forever grateful for the laboratory experience, not only for expanding my skill set in clinical medicine, but also for teaching me about the interpersonal nuances of the clinical work environment.

While in medical school, I became active in the student section of the American Medical Association, travelling to the national meetings every year. I enjoyed a rich experience of networking and learning from those in positions above me. One year, I put forth a policy about boating while intoxicated. Growing up near the Great South Bay of Long Island, I had witnessed the tragedies of those who drink while boating. I was nearly terrified the first time I had to speak in front of the entire national student convention at the national AMA meeting that year, as I presented my proposal as adopted by our New York Section.

The proposal passed the national level student body and made its way to the main floor. Eventually, the AMA adopted this proposal as an official policy of the AMA to be pushed out for a national policy agenda in public health. That was my first foray into healthcare policy, and I was hooked. Policy remains a passion of mine, even when it's local-level policy at the organizational level.

As I entered my third year clinical rotations, I decided to do my surgery rotation first to "get it out of the way," as I told my fellow students, firmly believing I was going to become a family practitioner or an internist/endocrinologist. I began my three-month rotation far from my school, where I had to stay on the hospital campus in student housing. I was shocked to learn that I loved surgery! I discovered that I naturally thought like a surgeon: see a problem, fix a problem. Granted, surgery can be complex, but the straightforward nature of surgical issues enticed me much more than the thought of attempting to long-term stabilize a brittle diabetic in their third DKA episode in a year.

Still, I kept to my plan to go into family medicine. I chose a two-week rotation in urology, figuring urological issues are common in family medicine. Once again, I was shocked at being swept up in a love for urology. However, I learned that it wasn't just the nature of the specialty but the mentor that made the difference! A good mentor can make or break a career decision, and that influence stays with me to this day.

I will never forget the urologist who took me under his wing for those two weeks. I followed him everywhere like a duckling from the moment he walked in until the moment he left the hospital. I absorbed everything he said, not just about urology, but about anything and everything. I watched everything he did, even his mannerisms in the operating room. It's amazing how two short weeks can have such a lifetime of influence. I still speak fondly of my mentor to this day.

A good mentor can make or break a career decision, and that influence stays with me to this day.

When the time came in my fourth year to choose my specialty, I went to my faculty adviser, who was a urologist. Once again, I began to have doubts, trying to choose between family medicine and urology. Like a true guide and mentor, he gave me some sage advice — not trying to influence me, but, instead, wanting me to determine the path that was right for me on my own. He told me to take a day off, go to my favorite park, and sit under a tree and think about what I truly wanted. Where could I see myself in the future? What would each path look like to me? So, I did just that, and I chose a life as a urologist.

I matched in urology, and once again, my choices guided me in my life path. I found that I had to move increasingly farther away from a major metropolitan center to find my peace. I was born and raised in the Bronx. My mother moved us to Long Island before my father succumbed to his illness knowing she did not want to raise two boys on her own in New York City. I spent a lot of time on Long Island and in New York city. I went to college outside of Boston, and I still enjoy Boston as one of my all-time favorite cities. However, returning to Long Island for medical school showed me how crowded and cramped even the Island was becoming.

I knew I had to leave the New York metropolitan area for calmer places. I chose Albany after meeting James Mandell, a pediatric urologist who was just taking over and rebuilding the urology program at Albany Medical Center in Albany, New York. His kindness and stalwart dedication gave me incredible confidence to want to train under him and the team he would build. I spent my five years in Albany training with some great people to whom I am incredibly grateful to this day.

As my time in Albany was coming to a close, I had to choose another position. As a urologist, the world was completely open to me, but I chose to stay in upstate New York for two reasons. First, I knew my wife's family was incredibly important to her. I remembered a presentation in medical school in which an adviser shared that eventually everyone moves to within 500 miles of their spouse's family. Staying close was paramount, Second, a fellow resident a year ahead of me in ENT told me, "Upstate New York is one of the best-kept secrets." I agreed in terms of the lifestyle, and it was what I wanted. So, I took a position with a solo urologist in Utica, New York — someone who would become not just a partner but also a great friend.

The first few years were probably standard for running a private practice. I had to learn all the things we were never taught in medical school, including finance, operations, risk management, compliance, coding, and human resources, among others. To bolster my knowledge, I took some business education classes and obtained an associate's degree. That wasn't enough for me. In 2003, I enrolled in a distance learning program for an MBA in healthcare administration from a school in California. Continuous education and self-improvement are key elements of the career journey and success, no matter the field.

During my first few years in practice, I realized that our local urologists from the main institutions in the area never held routine meetings, nor did they communicate in any meaningful collegial way. In addition, none of them fully participated in the governance structure at one of the main organizations. I took the initiative and called a dinner meeting for everyone under the auspices of a department meeting for one of the institutions. To my surprise, everyone showed up! My goal was to see how we could all integrate into a more collegial working relationship with a true departmental outlook at the larger organization.

During the dinner, I discussed how the department was near defunct and needed a chair to keep it running with representation at the medical executive committee level. Unanimously, I was volunteered by everyone around the table, mostly because no one else wanted the job. My "career" in medical staff leadership began that evening in 2003.

During this same time frame, from 2000 to 2004, I chose to give back to my community and country in two ways. First, I served in the United States Air Force Reserve in the 439th Aeromedical Squadron in Chicopee, Massachusetts, having joined shortly after completing my residency. I had an intense sense of duty growing up. My maternal grandfather served in the Kaiser's army in World War I. My father was ineligible to serve due to his diabetes, but my mother did work with the USO in her younger days. My brother joined the U.S. Navy on graduation from high school. I learned a great deal from my colleagues, fellow officers, my commander, and many of the NCOs (non-commissioned officers) with whom I served.

I was appointed the unit laboratory manager due to my experience as a medical technologist, and I was also appointed as the unit's HIPAA officer. Both experiences bolstered my skill set in leadership and oversight, as well as risk management and compliance. I will never forget and will always be fond of the friends and colleagues I made during my time in uniform.

The second way I decided to give back was by becoming an investigator as a volunteer position through our local humane society. I worked under the main investigator, learning a great deal about law enforcement. I still have my shield and sheriff's ID floating around my storage somewhere. Although it was rewarding, it was incredibly sad to witness the cruelty my fellow humans wrought upon the innocent animals who were supposed to be in their care.

I was only able to fulfill this role for 18 months before other duties became more pressing, forcing me to resign. I learned that any experience, no matter how short the time, is valuable in shaping our thoughts and feelings about the world and others around us.

I learned that any experience, no matter how short the time, is valuable in shaping our thoughts and feelings about the world and others around us.

Making the Hard Decisions

I realized early on in my career that a great deal of interaction and information exchange occurred with pharmaceutical, device, and diagnostic representatives, and I consider many of them friends. During my residency, and in the first year of my career, a medication for overactive bladder from Pharmacia was on the market. I became an early adopter, and I believed in the medication due to its efficacy and safety profile, which I touted as the best in class. Shortly after, at the end of 2000, the company released an extended-release version of the medication. One day, in early 2001, on seeing its improved benefits over the original immediate-release version, I jokingly said to the representative that the marketing slogan should be "the best just got better!" Little did I know that the representative took my statement back through channels, and a few weeks later, the vice president of sales for the company was on my doorstep to discuss using that slogan nationwide. My time as a consultant had begun.

I was signed to the speaker's bureau, travelling and speaking for the brand. When Pfizer acquired Pharmacia in 2003, I was included in Pfizer's speakers bureau, but my role expanded even further. I underwent formal public speaking training through Pfizer's corporate training program. I traveled to corporate headquarters in New Jersey to assist in training representatives. Unfortunately, the demands of clinical practice continued to increase, and much to my chagrin, I had to pare back on my consulting role. I had made many good friends during my tenure with Pfizer.

One day in 2008, when Pfizer was readying the launch of a newer formulation of its overactive bladder medication, having acquired the patent from a German company, I received a call from a friend of mine at Pfizer who was now in a national-level corporate position to offer me the position of medical director for that drug. It was my dream job! I had the qualifications, the background, the clinical skillset, the education (i.e., my MBA), but I had to say no. *It was the hardest decision I had made to date.*

> *Work-life balance is important in anyone's career, no matter what they choose to do.*

I had just gone through a rough divorce, and my children were young, only 2 and 4 years old. My work in the practice had forced me to sacrifice a great deal of time, including long hours of rounding, being in the office, and being on call nights and weekends. That poor work-life balance was a key element in destroying my marriage. In the divorce, I had structured my custody so that I could be more involved with my children. Based on my experiences, what led me to turn down the role with Pfizer was akin to the advice I gave my younger partner: "When you are on your deathbed, would you rather be known as a great urologist or a great dad?" It was that epiphany that forged a new internal standard against which I still judge many things, guiding me in my career since that sentinel event.

Work-life balance is important in anyone's career, no matter what they choose to do.

The years progressed, and in typical fashion for me, I continued my education. At the time, I wanted to learn more about emergency management to aid in my role as a medical staff leader. So, I completed an undergraduate certificate program that was offered free through FEMA in cooperation with Frederick Community College in Maryland. Getting back into education gave me the bug to learn more.

In 2017, the incoming president of the medical staff, who was also a friend of mine, asked me to consider being the vice-president of the medical staff at one of the local healthcare organizations that operated under a unified management service organization overseeing both institutional arms. I agreed, and was elected to serve under him. He was incredibly knowledgeable, having been president, interim medical director, and a JCAHO surveyor. I learned a great deal from him, but realized I needed to learn more to navigate the regulatory environment in healthcare, especially for larger organizations.

I had always considered law school, but, realizing I never wanted to practice law, chose to pursue a master's level degree. In 2018, I enrolled in an online master's program in legal studies that took me three years part-time to complete. I came away with a true love and appreciation for the law, and another skillset for my armamentarium. The learning improved my capabilities both as a medical staff leader and for the continued consulting work with outside organizations that I would provide.

Shortly before enrolling in the master's program for law, I became board-certified in obesity medicine. I was already board-certified in urology, so why would I seek a second board certification? My decision stems from a heated discussion I had with a bariatric surgeon at a department of surgery meeting shortly after I became vice-president of the medical staff. The issue was that the bariatric surgeons did not want to be part of the main general surgery call pool, preferring to create their own bariatric surgery call schedule.

We wrangled over the definition of bariatric medicine, and the head of the bariatric surgery program told me I didn't know what I was talking about. I knew I was right, and, as usual, I rose to the challenge. I decided to become board-certified in obesity medicine to purposely gain credibility in the field for future discussions, as well as to have an option for changing clinical focus of practice when I retired from urology.

Shortly after I became board-certified in obesity medicine, we had the same discussion at another department of surgery meeting with the same cadre of people. Once again, I was told I didn't know what I was talking about, but this time I pulled the "board-certified" card. I described the nature of bariatric medicine, including how it defied the definition that the bariatric surgeons tried to push.

Becoming board-certified was difficult, but it was the right thing to do to counter some significant issues at our organization. Sometimes in our careers, we face different forms of adversity. It is our decision whether to shrink away or rise to the challenge, tackling it head-on by amassing the needed tools to accomplish our goals and succeed.

> *Sometimes in our careers we face different forms of adversity. It is our decision whether to shrink away or rise to the challenge, tackling it head-on by amassing the needed tools to accomplish our goals and succeed.*

In 2014, the two healthcare organizations in the city merged under one MSO umbrella, but each maintained separate medical staff and nursing staff structures. In 2021, the Medical Staffs from the two major institutions merged into one singular staff with one set of Bylaws in anticipation of moving into one singular hospital.. I served as the vice-president of the newly formed unified medical staff, then served as the president of the medical staff (chief of staff) for the following two years.

During my tenure as the president of the medical staff, we had some turmoil with the chief physician executive divesting the duties of the CMO. While the organization did a CMO search, I met monthly with the CEO to discuss mutual concerns relevant to our positions. One particular day, my vice-president and the treasurer were with us as well. The CEO offered me the position of CMO. I had always considered being a CMO as a great stepping stone into administration and beyond. I had all the qualifications and knew the role well, in addition to understanding the regulatory environment. Again, I had to say no. This time, it was for different reasons.

I used the excuse that I was under a tightly controlled contract with my practice that had severe penalties if I were to leave my clinical position. That excuse was valid, but not my main concern. The bigger problem for me was that knowing the organization, both administrative and medical staff, I would be stepping into a nearly untamable quagmire. I didn't want to be part of that at all. Much to my disappointment, I had to decline.

I enjoyed my two years as president of the medical staff. I found myself thoroughly enjoying researching and creating policy for the organization as well as engaging in risk management, compliance, and quality processes regularly. I found myself diving into these arenas with zeal. One area I particularly enjoyed in my role was acting as a mentor and coach for medical students, residents, and colleagues. I enjoyed creating processes to groom future leaders and guiding medical students and younger colleagues on their career paths. This passion became the foundation for the coaching work I do and look forward to continuing.

When the two local hospitals closed and merged into the new facility in the city, my company, to which I was contracted and obligated, made the executive-level decision to pull my local branch practice out of that new hospital and begin covering a smaller facility. My partners and I were required to convert our staff privileges from the main hospital to a lower level without any responsibilities. I was heartbroken to leave many of my friends and obligations behind. However, with all things in life, as in our careers, any obstacle can become an opportunity!

Having more time away from administrative duties and coverage responsibilities, I decided to continue my educational journey.

I was already a member of the American Association for Physician Leadership (AAPL). With my newfound time, I wanted to advance further in my career on the leadership side, knowing my days in clinical medicine were coming to a close in the next few years. I completed my MPH to gain new skillsets to help me in potential roles in any healthcare industry, either public or private, and completed my Certified Physician Executive credential with the AAPL.

My years of leadership experience simmered over time, slowly like a stew — a slow cooking process filled with a medley of experiences that delivered me my own particular flavor of leadership that I want to continue sharing with others. I enjoy my work in consulting and coaching, as well as exploring the entrepreneurial side of medicine as I progress beyond the provisional patent for a urological device I designed with a close friend in a startup company we created. I plan to stay in clinical medicine for a few more years. Where the future leads, only the universe truly knows. As much as we think we are in control, oftentimes the universe says, "No, no! You're not going there!"

The only parting words I can offer, based on what I have learned over many years with numerous experiences, are that life often goes where you don't expect. Sometimes, the hardest decisions are the ones made for us, and not by us. Rise to a challenge constructively by bettering yourself and those around you. Be open to possibilities, see the positives, and find the opportunities. Sometimes, doing the right thing is the hard thing to do, but you need to do it anyway. Never stop learning, and if you're not happy, it's never too late to try something new or different.

> *Sometimes, the hardest decisions are the ones made for us, and not by us. Rise to a challenge in a constructive way by bettering yourself and those around you. Be open to possibilities, see the positives, and find the opportunities.*

In Their Words: Dr. Anonymous

TREMOR OR EARTHQUAKE

I remember it as if it were yesterday: my first time reading Guyton's textbook of physiology chapters on heart and lung mechanics. I immediately fell in love with the elegant models and couldn't get enough of it. As I progressed through medical school, I kept wanting to help patients. In my clinical rotations, I only saw doctors find problems whose solutions would cost more than what patients could afford. Meanwhile, in the surgery clinic, I saw patients grateful after their surgical recovery.

Consequently, I wanted to become a cardiothoracic surgeon. I reached an important milestone when I matched in a general surgery residency. The hours were long, the work was never-ending, but the learning was fulfilling and exciting. As I mastered the expected competencies during my first year of training, I continued to be assigned more complex cases in the operating room.

However, as I progressed in my duties as a surgical resident, a situation arose: I was shaking in the operating room. After my colleagues and I noticed the tremor, I started making lifestyle changes: sleeping more, keeping myself well hydrated, avoiding coffee, and limiting alcohol intake. Regardless of these changes, my tremor never went away. As a matter of fact, during my first vascular anastomoses, it became quite evident that I couldn't control it.

> *However, as I progressed in my duties as a surgical resident a situation arose: I was shaking in the operating room.*

I got a second opinion from a neurologist and was diagnosed with a mild case of essential tremor. At that moment, I learned a personal lesson in medicine: severity is relative, and a tremor could be mild for a teacher or an infectious disease doctor (like my uncles, who have it and only found out later in life) or a career-ending fault for an aspiring cardiothoracic surgeon like me.

157

The months following my neurological assessment, I did a lot of soul searching and decided to focus my career on providing non-surgical care to patients suffering from respiratory ailments. With the support of my program director and faculty, I successfully applied and matched at an internal medicine residency and later pursued a fulfilling career as a pulmonary and critical care doctor.

In His Words: Philip Horowitz, MD

SMASHBURGER

It was a few minutes to 1pm. My small lunchtime window was closing. I was enjoying the first few bites of my hamburger and fixings just the way I like it. "Dr. H," my front desk person announced over my phone, "there's a patient who just walked in and needs to speak to you."

I reacted violently, hurling the burger against the wall between two of the four monitors that lined the long desk in the small doc alcove. My first partner laughed, another gasped. It was out of character for me, the 65-year-old founder of an ophthalmology practice now in its 34th year of existence. It was, in retrospect, an inflection point. A classic sign of burnout in the life of a high-achieving son of immigrant parents.

> *I reacted violently, hurling the burger against the wall between two of the four monitors that lined the long desk in the small doc alcove.*

My Backstory

A Jersey boy, born in Somerville, to be exact. Parents: Laura, who left Kiev with her sister at age 9 — Jews forced out of Russia by the pogroms in 1918, and Saul, a Polish-born arrival to the U.S. in 1926. Both lived in New York City until my father was given a window-cleaning route in Somerville. I was their only child.

Saul was a taciturn man. Hard working. He didn't drive. Each day, he walked a mile or so to the heart of town carrying his pail, sponges, chamois, squeegees, and pole. He kept meticulous records, a green ledger book opened on the kitchen table, his suspenders down, a cutaway white shirt exposing his muscular arms. In winter, his hands were hardened and cracked. He was the disciplinarian. When Laura reported my misbehaving after he came home, I received a belt whipping across my buttocks. He died at age 43 in a Trenton "institution" when I was 12. He had been gone for months. Depression, perhaps? A diabetic-aided brain infection?

Laura was a superstitious woman who believed that any praise given to her child would invariably invite the evil eye of the universe into our house. I remember little affection. She died of metastatic breast cancer in 1958. She was 48.

I had two saving graces: my cousin GWM, 12 years my senior and daughter of my mother's sister; and my best friend MC's family. GWF always championed my smarts; she was my "person" for decades. MC's family was heaven-sent. They opened my eyes to art, music, the importance of scholastic achievement, and the world beyond me.

The High Achiever

I was home from college for the holidays in December 1957. I had turned 18 a month earlier. GWF, whom I always called Goldye, had a message for me. Dr. George Barber, the local surgeon who had operated on my mother four years earlier, wanted to speak to me. I met him in his office.

On the lighted X-ray box was my mother's film. I could see the missing shadow of her left breast, and he, wearing a crisp white smock, spoke to me, "Phil, those white specks filling both lungs, all lobes, are metastatic lesions. Your mother will die soon."

Goldye, her husband Sol, and her brother Jack had moved from New York City to run the window cleaning company for my mother. They had gotten an apartment and a live-in aide for my mother in another part of town. They saw her every day and attended to her every need.

> *On the lighted X-ray box was my mother's film. I could see the missing shadow of her left breast and he, wearing a crisp white smock, spoke to me, "Phil, those white specks filling both lungs, all lobes, are metastatic lesions. Your mother will die soon."*

Goldye took me to see her. The effects of a Halstead radical mastectomy were obvious. Her left arm was swollen. She looked thin and frail. There was little light in her eyes. I remember no words. I remember no tears.

I returned to Rutgers to take my exams for the first semester of my freshman year. I threw myself into my studies. My grades were stellar. Laura died April 8, 1958, the first night of Passover, a day or so after I was home for spring break. I remember the heavy rain during her funeral, the keening of her older sister Sonia, who had spirited my mother out of Russia. I held stoic at the graveside.

"But at any back I always hear/Time's Winged Chariot drawing near..." Andrew Marvel's poem "To His Coy Mistress"

Back at Rutgers, orphaned at 18, I went full-bore scholastic achiever. I expected time to run out on me, and I had no time to waste. I had always worked hard — first paying job at 14, and so it went. Phi Beta Kappa as a college junior, Alpha Omega Alpha as a Johns Hopkins Medical School junior, Hopkins medical internship, and Wilmer Ophthalmology Residency. I paid back Uncle Sam's military obligation with two years at the Staten Island Public Health Hospital (you know, conscription during those Vietnam War days).

Now What?

There was a brief period when I considered a career in academic medicine. I declined an offer to join an ophthalmology department in a teaching hospital in Chicago. Too little money. An offer to join a private practice in Baltimore was rescinded. My cousin Goldye loved the proximity of Staten Island and spending time with my first two young children. She made me promise to practice geographically close to her family.

My practice grew slowly at first, but I worked seven days a week, covered other practices in and around Cherry Hill, New Jersey, and prospered. Solo for the first 13 years, I added three partners and together we grew the practice to 10 doctors and three offices.

I hated Staten Island, but another doctor in the public hospital extolled the virtues of South Jersey, and that's where my band of four went. I started a solo practice there while still traveling three times a week to a moonlighting job I had found in Brooklyn, New York.

My practice grew slowly at first, but I worked seven days a week, covered other practices in and around Cherry Hill, New Jersey, and prospered.

Solo for the first 13 years, I added three partners and together we grew the practice to 10 doctors and three offices.

Back to the Hamburger

I realized that the stresses of working full-time at age 65 had gotten to me when I hurled the hamburger. I had the partners buy me out over the ensuing four years. I went to four days a week working for a percentage of my production in only one office. No on-call nights or weekends. I got to see my six grandkids grow up and traveled more with my second wife, Jackie. Fifteen years later, I retired at 80, just two weeks before COVID-19 was declared a worldwide pandemic.

I realized that the stresses of working full time at age 65 had gotten to me when I hurled the hamburger.

Final Thoughts

I believe it is a privilege to practice medicine and have people put their health and lives in your hands. When I started a solo practice, I knew that I wanted to be in full control of my fate. I spent a lot of time and effort with each patient. That care I gave was my biggest strength. But it was also my biggest weakness. I was never an efficient doctor, running on time and able to see more patients per hour. That productivity is increasingly necessary in today's world for a doc to be viable. We have more regulations heaped on us, face declining reimbursements, and must deal with Yelp reviews.

It ain't easy, but most doctors that I know still absolutely love what they do. Burnout is still a key reason why doctors leave the field. A therapist once told me, "Phil, you don't just put all that happened to you as a child in a box and it stays hidden there." So *that's* why I really threw that damn burger!

I believe it is a privilege to practice medicine and have people put their health and lives in your hands.

That care I gave was my biggest strength.
But it was also my biggest weakness.

In His Words: Kevin Klauer, DO, DJD

DESIRE

Leadership is a calling, not a vocation. Before you choose this path, I suggest reaching clarity on the question, "Why do I want to lead?" Career diversification, personal and professional growth, and service to others are just a few excellent reasons to seek leadership opportunities; there are so many more.

Leadership is a calling, not a vocation.

Pursuing leadership roles for the sake of "leading" in and of itself, being in charge, or for purely financial enrichment won't take you where you'd like to be, and will undoubtedly result in regret, disappointment, and frustration.

My thoughts on career diversification, pivots, or complete rebirths for physicians often anchor on leadership roles. The easiest pathway for those seeking opportunities is to be the solution to someone else's problem. You will find your greatest fulfillment where your experience as a physician matches an unmet need in someone else's world.

The easiest pathway for those seeking opportunities
is to be the solution to someone else's problem.

Sure, you can blow up your career and start all over again if you like. However, it makes more sense to build on your broad-based experience, applying what you know and what you can do through a new lens, via different optics, or in a different setting or healthcare-adjacent industry.

Personal and professional growth do not
happen without self-motivated challenge.

Personal and professional growth do not happen without self-motivated challenge. This is an incremental, iterative, and sometimes unrefined process. Trying new things, particularly in volunteer roles within medical affairs at your institution or group, can allow you to learn new things while exploring new career paths to find the best fit.

Seek opportunities, professional doors to walk through. Some doors may not be open to you today, but become your next opportunity months or years later, while others are wide open but don't inspire you to take the next step. The most desirable doors might include a hefty price of admission in the form of commitments such as time, additional education, and personal sacrifice. Your commitment to a new pathway must be commensurate with your passion and desire to gain access to that door or pathway calibrated by the likelihood you'll be invited through it. The juice needs to be worth the squeeze.

Keep knocking on doors, learning, and collecting knowledge. Someday, sooner than you may realize, the experience gained through this series of doors will be exactly what the person or organization on the other side of the very next door is desperately seeking.

Your commitment to a new pathway must be commensurate with your passion and desire to gain access to that door or pathway calibrated by the likelihood you'll be invited through it.

In Her Words: Karen J. Nichols, DO, MA, MACOI, MACP, CS-F

https://www.linkedin.com/in/karen-j-nichols-do-macoi-macp/

F.O.G. – READY OR NOT, HERE I COME

"Remember, you are in a fog," I said. He looked at me quizzically and responded, "And that is supposed to be helpful?"

My colleague had reached out after leaving his most recent employment to get some guidance on the best path forward. "Actually, I'm not talking about weather fog, I'm talking about an acronym, F.O.G. It stands for the following: You must have **Faith** that the **Future** will have **Options** and **Opportunities** to achieve your **Goals**. I shared that acronym in an article in the JGME, published in 2017." He embraced the significance of my advice, even though couched in an unusual acronym.

"Actually, I'm not talking about weather fog, I'm talking about an acronym, F.O.G. It stands for the following: You must have Faith that the Future will have Options and Opportunities to achieve your Goals."

This perspective has guided me through all of my careers. I have never been able to anticipate what was ahead for me, let alone plan for it. The following are summaries of my six careers.

First Career: Medical Technologist

I never intended to be a doctor; I never even considered that as an option. After being directed toward the medical technologist profession (pre-automation) while still in high school, I never wavered from that path.

My first job after graduating from Arizona State University was at Phoenix General Hospital (osteopathic); it was also my first exposure to the osteopathic profession. In about six months, the pathologist made me interim chief technologist. I'll never know why.

I had 60 employees, running a 24/7 lab in a 250-bed hospital. And I was 22 years old. Didn't see that coming!

The interim designation disappeared after a while. I had the opportunity (at night) to get a master's degree in management with a specialty in healthcare administration. I had decided that I was going to be a hospital administrator! I soon saw that it was a mistake and stayed on, running the lab. After about five years as chief, the pathologist called me in one day and said, "If there were anyone I would recommend to be a doctor, it would be you!" I didn't see that coming either!

Second Career: Physician

After taking more pre-med classes and the MCAT (twice) over two more years, off I went to Kansas City University-College of Osteopathic Medicine. It was soon clear to me that a career in internal medicine was the best choice for me. I completed an internship, which was required in those days, followed by the internal medicine residency in Tulsa.

In the final six months of the residency, I interviewed for practice opportunities at several places around the United States. Then one day, one of the IM docs who graduated from the residency program the year before me called to say the doctor he joined in practice in Arizona was moving to a practice in the mountains. Would I come join my old residency-mate? My husband and I were going to go home!

I must also point out my husband's incredible support throughout our entire marriage. He made these moves possible, changing from job to job to support us in the different cities. He managed many challenges without involving me, let alone even telling me what he had to do, so that I could focus on my studies. He then became the business manager of our three-doctor practice. I LOVED the practice and was soon department chair and then chief of staff of our 100-bed hospital. A 17-year run. And I was the first woman to be president of the Arizona Osteopathic Medical Association and the American College of Osteopathic Internists.

I must also point out my husband's incredible support throughout our entire marriage.

Third Career: Part-Time Medical Educator

Midwestern University/Arizona College of Osteopathic Medicine was founded in metro Phoenix about 12 years after I had been in practice. I had been teaching students on rotations for all that time and truly enjoyed the educational experience. So, I went out to the new campus and offered to assist where needed.

Fast forward to a phone call from the dean a few months later, offering me the part-time position of chair of internal medicine! My response? "Sure! What does the chair of IM do?" I soon found out. And a year later, I took on the part-time assistant dean for post-doc position, which meant I was meeting with hospitals around the state, eventually starting two new sponsoring institutions with over 100 residency positions. I had to learn about UME and GME curricula, standards, and finance, to name a few of the new topics that were required, to be able to handle these two positions.

Fourth Career: Full-Time Dean

One day, the president of Midwestern University scheduled a meeting between the two of us. When I got to her office, she said, "I hope you've come to accept a position, because I'm ready to offer you a job!" I said "yes," even though I wasn't sure what the job was!

I had heard that the dean in Chicago had not had his contract renewed. And sure enough, that was the job. When I told my husband the dean position was in Chicago, he said, "Well, drop in when you're in town!" Which I did.

We bought a condo in the Chicago suburbs, and I flew back to Arizona two or three times per month. We closed down the Arizona house every summer, and my husband spent those months in Chicago. Yes, we lived in two different cities for about seven months every year, yet it made our time together even more precious. What's more, most of my organizational meetings were already in Chicago, so that actually cut down on some travel.

I LOVED this job. Being the dean was certainly not easy. Sometimes it was heart- and gut-wrenching, and yet, just as with patient care, I knew it always mattered. I was dean for 16 years, then moved back to Arizona full-time for my next career opportunity.

Yes, we lived in two different cities for about
seven months every year, yet it made our
time together even more precious.

Fifth Career: ACGME Board Member and Chair

When the Single GME System was created, both AOA and the American Association of Colleges of Osteopathic Medicine had to nominate their first two board members. I chaired the AOA committee for that purpose. At the beginning of the first meeting, one of the committee members said, "We're throwing you off this committee." Before I could protest, he continued, "...because we are going to nominate you." Well, ok then.

Fast forward, I still remember my first ACGME board meeting. The only people I knew were the other three DOs on the 32-member board; I had no idea what the agenda items were about, or the processes, let alone the nuances. So I studied every document and watched and listened to learn. Four years later, I was elected as vice chair, followed by chair-elect, then two years as chair.

When I was elected vice chair, the handwriting was on the wall, that unless I messed up badly, chair-elect and chair were likely my next positions. So, I had a difficult decision to make as dean. I ultimately decided to step down as dean to devote full time to the ACGME. This turned out to be an excellent plan, as COVID hit soon after I became chair. While all our ACGME meetings became virtual, the number of meetings expanded exponentially. I found that I was running or participating in an ACGME meeting nearly every day that first year. I was an ACGME board member for eight years, terming off in 2022.

So, I had a difficult decision to make as dean.
I ultimately decided I had to step down as
dean to devote full time to the ACGME.

Sixth Career: Author/Speaker

I have been speaking about physician leadership for many years and am often asked, "What is the best book on physician leadership?" I always had two recommendations that I knew no one would follow because both books were over 500 pages long. No physician had the time to read that much material or even know where to start in those books. So, I wrote the book *Physician Leadership: The 11 Skills Every Doctor Needs to be an Effective Leader.* When people ask why I wrote the book, my answer is "Because no one else did." It is a concise presentation of the prime skills every physician needs to be a leader. It's available on Amazon in hard copy, as an eBook, and on Audible. And now I am on the speaking circuit at least monthly.

When I speak, I always tell the story about where I got the idea for the F.O.G. acronym. When living in the Chicago suburbs, I occasionally took the train to meetings downtown. One evening, returning home, the train stopped at my station in dense fog. You need to understand that those Metro trains can be 20 cars long, so sometimes you get off the train and can't even see the train station. On this day, I could literally only see two feet around where I was standing. Unable to see the cross street where I had parked that morning, I just started walking on down the sidewalk, not knowing whether I was going toward or away from my car. Finally, I came to a cross street that I recognized, and then I knew where I was. Thus, the basis for the acronym about the F.O.G: **Faith** that the **Future** will have **Options** and **Opportunities** to achieve your **Goals**. My point is, the car knew where it was. It was there waiting for me, ready to let me drive it home. I was the one in the fog.

> *My point is, the car knew where it was. It was there waiting for me, ready to let me drive it home. I was the one in the fog.*

So, upon reflection, my entire career evolved by just moving through the F.O.G. to a new place that was always there; I just didn't know about it. I didn't know what was ahead; I certainly didn't plan any of those careers. However, I did prepare, even if I wasn't aware of the future I was preparing for. Every step in my career has prepared me for a future step. Every experience has trained me for a future opportunity. Remember, "We're all in a F.O.G.!"

Every step in my career has prepared me for a future step. Every experience has trained me for a future opportunity.

(Side note from Pam Sullivan: I highly endorse Dr. Nichol's book and strongly recommend it to any physician embarking on a leadership journey. Her writing is highly authentic, allowing readers to easily connect with her experiences while gaining valuable knowledge, regardless of your leadership experience.)

In Her Words: Karen Raffery, MD, JD

https://www.linkedin.com/in/karen-hadam-614366/

TRIPLE THREAT

Doctor, Lawyer, Indian Chief.
So the nursery rhyme goes.
I was all three, now all three are me.

As an MD, JD, and a business entrepreneur, I was astonished to find that the question I was asked most was "Why?"

It is natural to question a path less taken. Sometimes the questions arose from curiosity, but occasionally from suspicion. Did she fail as a doctor? Did she fail as a lawyer? I occasionally felt like a Cold War spy, trusted in neither country. When we "change" professions, is the decision one of turning away or turning to something more? Perhaps not changing but evolving and pursuing our growth as professionals.

When we "change" professions, is the decision one of turning away or turning to something more?

As law school graduation grew near, it was time to formulate a career plan. Researching career coaches led me to an internationally known woman from London who had recently published a book. She graciously agreed to a call. I eagerly prepared for the discussion with my potential goals in mind, including hospital lawyer, business associate, and healthcare law.

Surprisingly, my coach was not interested in my potential job opportunities. Instead, she asked me to concentrate on my strongest skills. She concluded after careful consideration that I was a problem solver and that problem-solving should be my career.

In that message, I found perspective. There was a common thread in my pursuits. The conversation helped me reorganize my thought process about my profession. I learned to ignore the labels. It no longer mattered if I was a doctor, a lawyer, a business owner, or in administration. I brought knowledge, skill, and cumulative experience to help the person in front of me.

I learned in time to ignore the labels.

The driving motivations for my career were always the same. I had an intellectual curiosity that I longed to pursue and found great personal joy and satisfaction in those patients and clients whom I was privileged to serve.

In the end, being a Doctor, Lawyer, and Indian Chief is one.

One person who relentlessly pursues education both with books and experience in life.

One person who builds upon their skills and knowledge.

One person who is humbled by the privilege of sharing and caring for their fellow man.

One person who is humbled by the privilege of sharing and caring for their fellow man.

In His Words: Felix Reyes, MD, FCCP

https://www.linkedin.com/in/felix-reyes-105008197/

BEGINNINGS

I started my first attending job full of ideas, drive, and ambition. Due to immigration requirements, I was required to work in a medically underserved area for at least five years before becoming eligible for permanent residency in the United States. To fulfill this requirement, I chose a new community hospital in a growing community near Tucson, Arizona. I imagined that within those five years, I would be able to share my knowledge from a large academic institution while developing myself into a leader. My dream was to build multiple service lines while delivering great care for the local community.

At first, I interpreted the challenges I faced as being part of "growing into" my role as an attending or the "growing pains" of a brand-new hospital. But over the span of 24 months, I learned that these challenges reflected shortcomings in the organizational structure and a lack of organizational strategic thinking. As an example, I repeatedly proposed acquiring a piece of equipment that would allow us to do advanced bronchoscopy and perform 3–6 procedures per week or avoid interfacility transfers. The break-even point of this device at the current demand would be 30 months. Despite these arguments, I was unable to obtain institutional buy-in.

During these months, I began to develop a visceral sense of unease whenever I received a meeting invitation. What I previously met with excitement, I now met with somatization. Perhaps, I started to notice a misalignment between my employer's goals and mine.

During these months, I began to develop a visceral feeling of unease whenever I received a meeting invitation. What I previously met with excitement I now met with somatization.

At this point, believing that I was lacking skills, I became more active in professional societies such as the American College of Physicians and the American College of Chest Physicians, and took leadership classes to present my case to the hospital administration more effectively.

Trying to stay true to my values, I continued to bring innovative ideas, new service line proposals, and increasing efficiency. But for every step forward, we would take two steps backward; something that was previously "fixed" would go back to being "broken," and each new proposal was met with resistance from other stakeholders. I faced these daily challenges with resiliency. I can proudly say that although I never scored a victory, I never gave up.

In my third year of this position, I reflected on all the efforts made to move forward and decided that this institution did not align with my values. By this point, I had stopped visualizing a future with this organization. However, due to my immigration requirements, I felt trapped in this situation; I my next employer would need to meet strict requirements from the U.S. Department of State. To find a new job, I would have to walk in through the door with a big ask: "Could I task your organization with extra legal work before my first day of employment?"

During this time, my partner and the mother of our two-year-old son was interviewing for residency, and on match day, we learned that we would have to move out of this city. I embarked on a journey to find a new employer who could meet my specific requirements and that was located close to my family. I found several opportunities by tapping into my professional networks and directly contacting practices in my desired location.

Although I never found success in developing all the ideas I had for my first job, I was able to grow the network and the skills that helped me find a job that welcomes new ideas and allows me to be close to my family. Despite multiple setbacks, I learned that even in constrained situations, if you are strategic and continue to develop yourself, an opening will allow you to move forward.

Despite multiple setbacks, I learned that even in constrained situations, if you are strategic and continue to develop yourself, an opening will allow you to move forward.

175

In His Words: Pedro Rodriguez-Guggiari, MD, FACP
https://www.linkedin.com/in/pedro-rodriguez-guggiari-3a2ab6153/

EMBRACE CHANGE

Growing up as a compulsive daydreamer, far from knowing that medicine would become my road most travelled, I approached the world with a critical eye and a skeptical heart. With an older and wiser brother, I took to exploring science and labs, but I didn't revere it blindly. Rather, I found more questions while I took in and learned what I could. I questioned everything — experiments, conclusions, even the certainty with which authors seemed to speak.

During high school, I quickly gravitated toward art and writing. I read with curiosity and reveled in the uncertainties that each philosopher or poet found themselves in, and at the risk of sounding presumptuous, making them more akin to my journey. In my home country of Paraguay, there is no such thing as pre-med or an undergraduate degree. So, I delved headfirst into medical school, knowing well that there would still be uncertainties.

As my generation welcomed the '90s, in the flurry of AIDS and the Gulf War, evidence-based medicine (EBM) was becoming a thing. I studied immunology with professors who encouraged us to question everything. I found myself reluctantly thrown into leadership roles (most likely because others didn't want to take it on). From exploring the field to speaking as our class representative, I fended off boredom easily, a trait that lingers to this day.

As soon as I could, I took a role as a teaching assistant in socio-anthropology. That helped me look not just at the patient or the person, but society as a whole and how we function. The first class consisted of debates based on our understanding of the movie "Dancing with Wolves." It is fascinating how we can't get along, yet we have to define a common pathway for whatever people embrace as success. From that first teaching assistantship onward, I was hooked and continued to assist in many other courses — not because I thought I knew more than the junior students, but because it pushed me to learn and grasp a deeper understanding.

*It is fascinating how we can't get along, yet
we have to define a common pathway for
whatever people embrace as success.*

In our third-world country, folklore taught us that if you felt rewarded honing your technical skills, surgery would be your calling. At that time, surgery was truly a passion of mine. However, an internist was seen as a most virtuous clinician (which sadly, is untrue for some colleagues today).

When a professor of internal medicine, unhappy with my answers or thought process, assessed with certainty that I would become a skilled surgeon one day, I considered that another challenge to rise to. After a rotational internship in rural medicine, I knew that resources and experiences in the country were limited, as was a more formally structured postgraduate training, and I needed to pursue USMLEs. Therefore, I relocated to New York City, where after completing my USMLEs, I found myself counseling and tutoring international medical graduates at Kaplan Educational Centers until the time of my match and my formal residency training.

*After a rotational internship in rural medicine,
I knew that resources and experiences in
the country were limited, as was a more
formally structured postgraduate year
training, and I needed to pursue USMLEs.*

Once I began my residency, I was again eager to learn through teaching. A Spaniard colleague of mine and I set up an informal course, "Medical Spanish for Residents," which our peers welcomed. In my third year, I was chosen to be one of three chief residents.

The challenges brought on by the events of 9/11 shaped me greatly, not just as a leader but also as a person. I witnessed a pulmonary fellow of Iranian background crying after suffering discrimination from his own patients. I also saw patients who felt discriminated against for their background, belief, or orientation. I learned another facet of our most human career and calling:

supporting our suffering community and building resilience among our peers.

I witnessed a pulmonary fellow of Iranian background crying after suffering discrimination from his own patients, as well as patients who themselves felt discriminated against for their background, belief or orientation.

Honing My Leadership Skills

Although I was accepted into the pulmonary and critical care fellowship I was most interested in, a friend contacted me about a position in Arizona. I envisioned a stereotypical cowboy town, yet found myself relocating to Peoria, the fifth-largest growing city in the United States. Having decided that I was unlikely to return to Paraguay anytime soon, I embarked on the journey of private practice – traditional style with inpatient and outpatient duties.

As the position was in an underserved area, the workload tended to be brutal, and my peers in similar situations struggled equally. I developed a keen sense of adjusting schedules and workloads to reduce our risk of being overworked or burned out, while at the same time improving our services to our patients.

Despite my every effort, I lost the wager against the productivity machine, and nothing was ever enough for our employers. At least, that is how I saw it. I transferred to another budding practice where we eagerly gained a contract with a cancer specialty hospital in Phoenix and developed not just their inpatient hospitalist service but also their comprehensive Internal medicine clinic, which functioned for the intake of complex patients, chronic condition management, and a quasi-urgent care for patients and even their out-of-state relatives. Managing patient services, working with other staff and specialties, while maintaining provider satisfaction, was again a cornerstone of my activities.

Unhappy with how the practice I managed was conducting their affairs, I opened my own private practice, which I grew to eight providers in three offices. I honed my business skills while managing a larger population of patients and staff. Then, amid strained relationships with payers regarding in-patient care management, I opted to join the hospitalist service at Banner Health, soon taking over as chief of medicine and then chief of staff at our hospital.

Boy, did I learn a lot in the new position! I also learned a lot in the hard school of the COVID pandemic. After some blows from the healthcare environment and economic events, I was invited to be the associate program director at a new internal medicine residency and focus on developing primary care doctors, training physicians to be the best internists they can be. I feel privileged to have the opportunity to form these young and brilliant colleagues, since they will face challenges we have not yet dreamed of. They may also find that the only constant thing in the universe is change.

From skeptic to steward, from student to teacher — I didn't choose medicine with certainty. But I stay and embrace with conviction.

And that has made all the difference.

From skeptic to steward, from student to teacher
— I didn't choose medicine with certainty.
But I stay and embrace with conviction.

And that has made all the difference.

In His Words: Geogy Thomas, MD, FAAFP, MBA
https://www.linkedin.com/in/geogy-thomas-a564996b/

EXPECTATIONS

"When are you going to be done with this phase and become a real doctor?"

As painful as those words were to hear, I understood where my dad was coming from. He was the first generation in our Asian family who had worked hard to see his son pursue dreams and the aspirations that were never within his reach. He hoped to see his son become an affluent physician, preferably a specialist in a sprawling metropolis.

Instead, I had chosen to be a country doc serving in rural Appalachia. Despite the fact that I was trained at a renowned family medicine residency in Ventura, California, my dad would always see me as a general practitioner living among poor rural folk.

At the time of this confrontation, my family and I had been living in rural Tennessee for seven years where I was a family physician, providing full-spectrum care, including surgical OB. I had also been a medical director for our community health center with three rural sites, caring for over 10,000 patients in our region, where 25% of our patients lived below the poverty level. Yeah, being a country doc for a bunch of poor white people was not an Asian parent's dream for their son.

Yeah, being a country doc for a bunch of poor white people was not an Asian parent's dream for their son.

If I were to be honest, it was not mine either.

Growing up, I refused to say I wanted to be a physician because I knew that was exactly what my dad wanted of me. I excelled in math and sciences but refused to entertain the thought of medicine as a career. It was at a missions conference at the University of Illinois when I was a freshman that I came face-to-face with the profound poverty, injustice, and hopelessness that many people around the world faced. It was at this conference that I felt called to care for those who were hurting physically, emotionally, and spiritually, and to use medicine as a bridge into their lives.

I finished undergrad and then went directly to medical school at the University of Illinois, Rockford, where I met and married my beautiful bride, Jessie. She, too, was a South Asian but grew up in New York.

When it was time to choose a residency, I was convinced I needed to go into family medicine. I loved the variety that family medicine offered. Your patients come in all sizes, ages, genders, and backgrounds. Their needs range from physical to emotional, mental, and preventive. Your care includes acute, chronic, and preventive. Family docs can add on procedural, family planning, and specialty care.

Another compelling reason that I chose residency in family medicine was that as a family physician, you have the opportunity to take care of entire families, from the tiniest of infants to the oldest of grandparents. It's not for everyone, but it was definitely for me.

The decision to pursue family medicine landed us in Ventura, California, which was known for its "cowboy family medicine program" that equipped providers to go to the hard, underserved areas. Ventura's residency was renowned for providing family docs with extra training, including c-sections, appendectomies, and colonoscopies.

The program included long, grueling work hours (this was before the 80-hour work week limit), call every 3–4 nights, the lowest resident salaries in the nation, and a high divorce rate among its residents. Yes, sign me and my new bride up! All joking aside, Jessie and I felt called to serve in a place with little to no access, and we knew that this intense training was what we needed to be equipped to serve well. It would be the best ROI for our future.

All joking aside, Jessie and I felt called to serve in a place with little to no access and we knew that this intense training was what we needed to be equipped to serve well. It would be the best ROI for our future.

The training definitely lived up to its reputation for its long hours and low pay, but the program itself brought some of the most amazing faculty and staff together to demonstrate how to care for the most vulnerable people. The residency serves the county's large population of migrant workers, public aid recipients, and veterans, providing ample medical training for its newly minted doctors, and also giving them a front row seat to the suffering of people. It's in this seat that residents learn empathy, compassion, and advocacy.

Despite the brutal training, we loved our time in Ventura. It was paradise. Ventura is situated on the coast, boasts 70-degree weather year round, and is absolutely beautiful! But, after three precious years, it was time to move on.

A Change of Plans

Our intent was to move overseas, but I still had two years of NHSC scholarship to pay off, which meant that I needed to serve in a rural or inner city of the United States. A recruiter contacted me, promising that he had the perfect job for me. I could be a full-spectrum family doc, providing outpatient and inpatient care, including surgical OB, ultrasounds, vasectomies, and ICU care. It did sound perfect except for one thing: It was located in rural Tennessee, the heart of Appalachia. I had visions of burning crosses, the Beverly Hillbillies, and Doc Hollywood playing through my head. There is no way I would take my wife and two small children to Tennessee! I finally relented and agreed to an onsite interview.

They looked different from my patients in California, but still struggled the same with the realities of poverty, inequity, and brokenness. (Clearly, I had my own prejudices to repent of.)

Was I humbled. We fell in love immediately. The clinics were located in the majestic Appalachian mountains. The practice was exactly what I trained for. The people were precious. They looked different from my patients in California, but struggled the same with the realities of poverty, inequity, and brokenness. (Clearly, I had my own prejudices to repent of.)

I signed on immediately without interviewing anywhere else. My attendings in Ventura were less than impressed. My new job in Appalachia would have me working 70 hours per week, on call every 2–4 days, and pay me less than 60% of the national average for family physicians. Clearly, I have a thing for low-paying jobs. I was planning to go overseas, where I would get paid a fraction of my new salary.

So for the next two years, I hunkered down as a family doc in a small town of 2,500 people, providing care in the clinic and in the hospital. My Ventura training was quite handy, as I performed crash C-sections, ultrasounds, intubations, and vasectomies. I was having the time of my life, doing what I loved — so much so that when my two-year NHSC commitment was completed, we decided to stay.

We built a house, homeschooled our three kids, got involved in the community, and pastored a church. Everyone knew who we were (it's kinda obvious being brown in a sea of white people) and treated us so kindly. Going to Walmart became increasingly cumbersome because patients would stop us to update me on their mamaw's cancer, or show me a rash or tell me how much the baby I had delivered for them had grown. Walmart was quickly becoming an extension of my clinic. The solution: Jessie took one cart and did the real shopping; I took the kids in another cart and did my Walmart rounds, visiting patients along the way.

I was having the time of my life, doing what I loved so much so that when my two-year NHSC commitment was completed, we decided to stay.

In many ways it was an idyllic setting. However, a dark reality was settling in on rural medicine. Staggering poverty, lack of jobs, and poor school systems were setting the stage for some of rural America's toughest years ahead. The Norman Rockwell years were over. Like all Americans, those who live in rural areas have struggled with uncontrolled chronic illness, mental health issues, dental decay, and abuse of all kinds. The difference is that rural America is out of sight, out of mind. Their issues, their struggles, their voices are rarely heard.

The Scourge of OxyContin

When we moved to Appalachia in 2000, OxyContin had just entered the market. Purdue Pharmacy was marketing specifically to Appalachia, ready to profit from vulnerable, hard-working folk. I recall pharmaceutical reps touting that "OxyContin is NOT addictive." I recall reps leaving glossy brochures and graphs that touted pain relief without addiction (all later found to be false, doctored by Purdue). I recall reps warning me that I would be responsible for creating drug addicts by not prescribing Oxy to my patients needing pain relief, that I'd be pushing them to go on the streets and get heroin instead.

Our phones and clinics were flooded with angry patients who demanded these pain meds. I recall one mom who was adamant that her 16-year-old daughter needed OxyContin to help her with pain from her UTI. Many of these patients transferred to other clinics that saw profit in catering to this crowd.

> *I recall pharmaceutical reps touting that "OxyContin is NOT addictive." I recall reps leaving glossy brochures and graphs that touted pain relief without addiction (all later found to be false, doctored by Purdue). I recall reps warning me that I would be responsible for creating drug addicts by not prescribing Oxy to my patients needing pain relief, that I'd be pushing them to go on the streets and get heroin instead.*

I truly believe that in poverty medicine, you can make a decent living if you do it well and respect your patients. At the same time, you can make a killing if you do medicine poorly, taking advantage of desperate people. This is exactly what unfolded right in front of our eyes.

Sensing a lucrative opportunity, predators started swarming to Appalachia, opening up "pain clinics" that at best were pill mills running a legalized drug operation, preying on the desperation of our communities. These pill mills started popping up all around us, promising relief to people in pain while painting practices like mine as insensitive and uncaring. Many of these clinics were cash-only, seeing patients monthly for $400 per visit.

Patients would leave with a script for one month's supply of Oxy 40 mg TID, Klonopin 2mg TID, and gabapentin 600mg TID. This extremely dangerous and highly addictive combo was commonplace for most patients, including pregnant women! The reality was that many of those patients were taking just a fraction of those meds and selling the rest to pay for their habits, but also, frankly, to pay for life itself. Talk about a pyramid scheme! It was survival for some, escape for others, and a jackpot for the entrepreneurial predators.

As the pill mills became more popular, our practices initially experienced some respite from patients demanding pain meds. That quiet was short-lived as our OB practice started seeing large numbers of pregnant woman coming for their OB care who were using substances during their pregnancy. As family physicians, we did not feel comfortable taking care of this high-risk population. We would quickly refer them to high-risk OB in Knoxville, one hour away, only for those patients to no-show for their referral and eventually come to our local hospital in active labor. Within 48 hours of delivery, those precious babies would start showing signs of withdrawal, crying incessantly with severe tremors and tight muscle tones.

One morning on rounds, a mom whose baby I had delivered the night before showed off how "advanced" her baby was. She held her baby's hands while the baby stood straight up on the bed. The mom was convinced this child, less than 24 hours old, was ready to walk. In reality, the newborn was exhibiting signs of severe withdrawal; his muscles were so stiff and spastic that it looked like he could stand up on his own. Withdrawing babies such as these were quickly transferred to the University of Tennessee for NICU care. They stayed there for up to six weeks, costing the state $65,000 per child.

Opioid prescriptions in Campbell County were five times above the national average, putting us on the map as the Opioid Red Zone. In time, overdoses became commonplace. The addicts who did not die walked around like zombies, unable to work or care for their families. Grandparents were raising their grandkids. It seemed as if a whole generation of people was missing.

We realized that as a practice, we could not stand on the sidelines any longer as the drug epidemic ravaged our communities. Patients were getting sicker, people were dying, families were being destroyed, and crime was going up. We decided to partner with the University of Tennessee to develop programs to help women detox during pregnancy, with the hope of giving these women a chance to reclaim their futures.

Although we did not want to exchange one drug for another, we started offering buprenorphine, hoping to wean women completely off their opioid addictions. The program began to see some success, especially as we engaged behavioral health counseling, wraparound services, and strong accountability.

> *As a practice we realized we could not stand on the sidelines any longer as the drug epidemic ravaged our communities.*

As we developed this program, I began to realize how complicated and, at times, hopeless it was to fight the healthcare winds. Clearly, we were trying to save patients who were drowning downstream while opportunistic systems were pushing innocent people into the waters upstream. (A huge shout out to Dan Heath's powerful book *Upstream,* which helped me process this struggle.) This was exhausting. Sure, we were providers and saving lives is what we do best, but we need people to go upstream and fix systems and right the wrongs.

The Next Step: The Business Side

In 2015, I decided to get my MBA. They don't teach you business skills, strategy, or efficiency in med school. To truly understand healthcare costs and impact, I needed further training.

Earning my MBA helped me view healthcare from a different perspective. It was a lens that exposed inefficiencies and focused on strategy and finance, helping me to identify problem areas in the system. It was no longer about simply providing healthcare but rather about delivering it efficiently and with excellence. With more tools in my toolbox, I found myself traveling upstream, identifying issues and developing systems and safeguards. We added new service lines like school health, behavioral health, and dental services.

The growth was exactly what our community needed, providing care that our patients could not otherwise access. Unfortunately, the growth also exposed our financial cracks. It was 2018, and one out of four health centers was in dire financial straits. Our clinic was no exception. By 2019, we found ourselves two payroll cycles away from closing, and our board asked me to step in as CEO.

Honestly, I never wanted to be a CEO and definitely not one for a sinking Titanic. After a lot of prayer and counsel, I reluctantly agreed to serve as the interim CEO. I felt responsible for my staff, my patients, and my community. As a physician, I could land a job anywhere; the rest of my staff did not have that option. I had to stay. I had to lead. I had to find a way out of this desperate situation.

Getting my MBA helped me look at healthcare from a different perspective. It was a lens that exposed inefficiencies and focused on strategy and finance, helping me to identify problem areas in the system.

Fortunately, we had an amazing CFO whom we had hired the year prior when we started to sense the impending doom. He and I comprised our entire executive team and got to work immediately, trying to right the ship. We quickly realized that we were conducting business as a mom-and-pop shop. We had to modernize our business model. We needed to update our systems, demand better reimbursements from our payers, diversify our revenue streams, and require increased accountability. "No money left behind" was our war cry.

If becoming the CEO of a dying clinic wasn't hard enough, imagine taking the helm during a pandemic! COVID hit three months after I assumed the CEO position. Not only did we have to restructure our entire business model, we needed to do it with the world on fire. To add insult to injury, our local hospital, the only safety net for our community, closed its door permanently. Tennessee hospitals were closing at record rates, following the national trend of rural hospitals being unable to afford the high cost of healthcare for their low-income residents. *Talk about building a plane, while in flight, while getting shot at.* That was our world.

> *If becoming the CEO of a dying clinic wasn't hard enough, imagine taking the helm during a pandemic! COVID hit three months after I had assumed the CEO position.*

There was one silver lining: COVID funds. These funds helped us get by while we fixed our systems. It bought us time. We were able to turn our finances around by 2021, and embraced our new goal: to be the Provider of Choice for our patients and the Employer of Choice for our community.

For our patients, we wanted to be their medical home, focused on offering high-quality care. We wanted to be a place where they knew they were loved and would get the best care possible. We hoped to improve access, allowing patients to get the care they needed, when they needed it the most, by a team they could trust.

For our staff, we wanted to be a place where they knew they would earn a competitive salary and benefits, where they enjoyed a culture of peace, and they were part of something sacred.

With the hospital closing, that goal became much harder. Patients now had to travel almost an hour for diagnostic testing, emergency/inpatient care, or even to deliver their babies. Specialists were a hot commodity. Patients often had to wait 9–12 months to get an appointment with a rheumatologist or neurologist and, again, with a one-hour commute. Many patients could not afford the gas and didn't have reliable cars to make the trek. Patients would delay diagnosis, suffer in pain, or just concede to a miserable existence due to access issues.

With so many of our patients facing such challenges to access essential health services, we new we had to find a solution. As I watched my patients struggle with access, I developed a vision for a one-stop healthcare experience. Around that time, an old Walmart space with about 65,000 square feet became available in our community. We immediately began strategizing on how to make this space a comprehensive medical/dental home for our community.

We were guided by the "triple aim": the final product had to be beautiful, had to be efficient for patients and staff, and had to make financial sense. The goal was to meet the challenges of delivering quality healthcare in rural America.

A year and a half later, Dayspring Regional Health Center, a 65,000-square-foot comprehensive medical center is a reality. The new center has designated spaces for family medicine, pediatrics, women's health, behavioral health, and dental services. To bolster the "one-stop healthcare" concept, the center has a robust diagnostic center with CT, MRI, US, and X-ray; a lab; and a pharmacy. The facility also houses physical therapy, chiropractic services, medical massage, and a concierge tele-specialties service.

Having secured the comprehensive medical center I had long envisioned, I felt like we had moved the needle. We were making strong gains to be the Provider of Choice, Employer of Choice. Our beautiful new medical mall would allow us to add "Community of Hope" to our mantra, as the site reminds people that the story of Appalachia is not done. There is great beauty in these hills.

A New Chapter

After the building was completed in 2024, I chose to officially step down from the CEO position. I was tired. I had been the CEO and CMO during a pandemic and financial implosion. I had been seeing patients two days per week while building a medical-dental mall. Actually, I was exhausted.

As much as I loved being the CEO, I was ready for rest and hopefully a new adventure. I was blessed to be able to hand the reins to my CFO/COO who had been instrumental in turning our practice around in 2020.

After the building was complete in 2024, I chose to officially step down from the CEO position. I was tired.

Twenty-five years later, as I look back, I recognize my journey has taken me away from a lucrative position in California, away from our families in Chicago and New York. This journey has taken me away from the "glamorous" opportunities in suburbia.

Instead, I was "called" to a different journey, to walk alongside a population of the United States whose voices have been forgotten or simply not heard – the rural poor. I was called to serve a group of people, who, despite their poverty, demonstrate their tremendous gratitude with a jar of jelly, a basket of vegetables, and occasionally a bottle of moonshine.

> *Instead, I was "called" to a different journey, to walk alongside a population of the United States whose voices have been forgotten or simply not heard – the Rural Poor. I was called to serve a group of people who, despite their poverty, demonstrate their tremendous gratitude, with a jar of jelly, a basket of vegetables, and occasionally, a bottle of moonshine.*

I was called to serve a group of people who, despite their own paralyzing battles, are the first to extend a warm hug and a sometimes toothless smile. I was brought to a place where my patients are my friends and my family, to a place where Walmart and church are extensions of my medical offices.

My dad lived with us for about five years before he passed away in 2023. He had had a stroke, and it was too much for him and my mom to live by themselves in Chicago. Of course, he came kicking and screaming, not wanting to leave the big city to come to our hick town. He eventually settled into country living.

One afternoon, I approached my dad as he was sitting on the porch, gazing at the mountains like a good Southerner in summer. I shared my concerns. We needed to move. As my dad's health continued to decline and with our hospital closing, it was no longer safe to stay in Jellico. We needed to be in a city with more healthcare options. By the way, that is what privilege sounds like in a rural community.

His response was quick and direct. "No. We are not moving."

"But why?" I felt myself regressing into my teen self while trying desperately to cling to every bit of authority I had as a physician, caretaker, CEO, and adult son.

"Son, these people need you. They can't move like you and I can. You cannot leave them. More importantly, you need them. You are who you are because of how this community has shaped and molded you to be the leader you are today. Geogy, when you and Jessie decided to move here many years ago, I fought you because I did not understand how important and precious the work you would be doing was. Now I understand, and we cannot leave."

In Her Words: Ijeoma Uche, MD, PharmD, FACP

juuche@yahoo.com

KEEPING THE FAITH

I have often considered myself a pluripotent stem cell capable of achieving anything in life with the right training and exposure. Thus, it has been a journey of self-discovery to unlock the potential that lies within.

The idea that I could achieve anything engendered the assumption that I would be successful in life. Looking back, I wish I had taken the time to define success for myself. Instead, I seem to have taken on a societal definition of success. There are many societies in the world, and they surprisingly differ in terms of what they view as success. If you consider yourself an American female, then success usually equates to being physically beautiful (the skinnier the better), smart, well-liked (think followers on social media), and of course having the financial means to acquire things (the more "toys" the better). To earn superwoman status, success would mean that your marriage is near perfect (at least on the outside), and your children are at least enviable.

> *Looking back, I wish I had taken the time to define success for myself. Instead, I seem to have taken on a societal definition of success.*

This ideal of perfection comes along for the ride in our careers. Despite my credentials as a pharmacist, physician, clinician educator, and mentor, I seem to always be grasping professionally, never quite reaching that euphoric sentiment that translates into "I have finally arrived."

I recall one of my pharmacy school professors stating that only a fraction of our class would pass pharmacokinetics, one of the toughest classes in the curriculum. If I could not complete pharmacy school, how could I journey onward to medical school?

Born in the United States but raised in West Africa, I returned to the United States at a young age to attend college with the intent to become a physician. The idea of being a pharmacist never even entered my head. After completing my undergraduate studies at the University of California, Berkeley, I applied to several medical schools. At the urging of my parents, I also applied to pharmacy school.

As fate would have it, I did not gain acceptance to any of the medical schools, but I was accepted into the only pharmacy school to which I applied. My initial reaction was that I'd rather retake the MCAT instead of going to pharmacy school. Once again at the urging of my parents, I proceeded to pharmacy school because as my parents put it, "a bird in hand is worth two in the bush." Deep down in my heart, I never really gave up the idea of being a physician, so decided (but didn't share) that I would complete pharmacy school and then pursue medical school.

Thus, the declaration that only a fraction of the class would pass pharmacokinetics and subsequently graduate pharmacy school was a major disruptor to my plans. I had to graduate from pharmacy school. I had to succeed by any means possible. I began searching for a higher power. By this, I mean something or someone that renders obstacles powerless and assures victory. It was at this time that I gained a deeper understanding of my Christian faith and developed a personal relationship with God.

Fast forward two and a half years later. I graduated from pharmacy school with board licensure and multiple job offers. After practicing as a hospital pharmacist for four years, I gained admission to medical school. During the preclinical years in medical school, I worked locum tenens as a pharmacist to pay for medical school tuition. I graduated from medical school and passed all USMLE licensing exams on my first attempt.

> *I tried to settle into life as an endocrinology fellow, but could not help the growing sense of unease within....I found the courage to act according to my convictions and take the less-traveled road.*

Choosing a specialty was tough because I enjoy every aspect of medicine. Ultimately, my penchant for analytical thinking coupled with an inclination for a less procedurally oriented specialty led me to internal medicine, followed by a fellowship in endocrinology, a seemingly good fit.

I tried to settle into life as an endocrinology fellow, but could not help the growing sense of unease within. The political constructs around reproductive medicine, transgender medicine, and synthetic applications of sex hormones led to conflicts with my Christian faith. I decided to leave my endocrinology fellowship after one year. Today, I do not doubt that this was one of the best decisions I have made professionally. I found the courage to act according to my convictions and take the less-traveled road.

Trying to pick up the pieces of my professional life after exiting the endocrinology fellowship was not easy. I began by working locum tenens. It was a welcome change to be able to set my own schedule and take a few months off to get much-needed rest. I was surprised by the immense opportunities for locum tenens work available in virtually all physician specialties. Working locum tenens meant having to adapt quickly to new and rapidly changing environments, such as electronic medical records (EMRs), office staff, work schedule, expectations, and patient load/mix. Over time, I got better at "hitting the ground running" with each locum tenens assignment.

I continued working as a locum tenens while patiently seeking permanent employment that is burnout-proof. I thought back to previous positions I held to remind myself which aspects of those positions I liked. Could I really have a great career in medicine without being overworked and burned out? As I transition from an early-career to a mid-career physician, I have become more interested in blended roles. The ideal job would be one that combines clinical duties with teaching responsibilities and leadership roles. I want to have a voice in making decisions that directly affect how I work. I want to keep learning and growing clinically. I want to help shape the future generation of physicians. I enjoy managing complex cases in hospital medicine and advocating for patients with difficult psychosocial dynamics.

I began applying for permanent academic hospitalist positions across the country. As I interviewed for positions, I was surprised that employers were willing to accommodate and even custom-fit positions to meet my preferences. The combination of clinical experience, the ability to adapt rapidly to change, and the courage to turn challenges into growth opportunities has become my brand.

I am currently employed as a faculty physician in a well-established residency program where I supervise residents and medical students on inpatient rotations. My schedule consists of 14 days on followed by 14 days off. I participate on select committees related to resident education and hospital administration. I mentor trainees and early-career physicians. My clinical duties take place in a large safety net hospital with a superb mix of complex cases interspersed with commonly encountered conditions.

I am not sure if I have reached my zenith in terms of career satisfaction. However, this is the closest I have come to it. I am learning to make decisions that allow me to live my true self rather than subscribe to societal or external pressures that define success. The end result is a path that is uniquely my own.

I am learning to make decisions that allow me to live my true self rather than subscribe to societal or external pressures that define success. The end result is a path that is uniquely my own.

www.ingramcontent.com/pod-product-compliance
Lightning Source LLC
Chambersburg PA
CBHW061214220326
41599CB00025B/4637